MARC
IBI
FORMENTERA

with Local Tips
*The author's special recommendations are
highlighted in yellow throughout this guide*

There are five symbols to help you find your way around this guide:

Marco Polo's top recommendations – the best in each category

sites with a scenic view

places where the local people meet

places where young people get together

(100/A1)
pages and coordinates for the Road Atlas
(U/A1) *coordinates for the City Map inside back cover*

MARCO ⊕ POLO

Travel guides and language guides in this series:

Alaska • Algarve • Amsterdam • Australia/Sydney • Bahamas • Barbados
Berlin • Brittany • California • Canada • Channel Islands • Costa
Brava/Barcelona • Costa del Sol/Granada • Côte d'Azur • Crete • Cuba
Cyprus • Dominican Republic • Eastern Canada • Eastern USA • Florence
Florida • Gran Canaria • Greek Islands/Aegean • Ibiza/Formentera • Ireland
Istanbul • Lanzarote • London • Mallorca • Malta • Mexico • New York
New Zealand • Normandy • Paris • Prague • Rhodes • Rome • San Francisco
Scotland • South Africa • Southwestern USA • Tenerife • Turkish Coast
Tuscany • USA: Southern States • Venice • Western Canada

French • German • Italian • Spanish

*Marco Polo would be very interested to hear your
comments and suggestions. Please write to:*

North America:
Marco Polo North America
70 Bloor Street East
Oshawa, Ontario, Canada
(B) 905-436-2525

United Kingdom:
GeoCenter International Ltd
The Viables Centre
Harrow Way
Basingstoke, Hants RG22 4BJ

Cover photograph: Transglobe: Herbst
Photos: J. Gläser (27, 32, 46, 60, 76, 79); K. Kallabis (22, 44, 62, 80);
Lade: Mehlig (56), Murillo (50), Vidler (4, 8); Mauritius: Cash (37, 67), Hubatka (68, 99);
T.P. Widmann (12, 14, 20, 24, 28, 54, 70, 73, 82)

2ⁿᵈ revised edition 2000
© Mairs Geographischer Verlag, Ostfildern, Germany
Authors: Patrick Müller and Rolf Schwarz
Translator: Michael McCarroll
English edition 2000: Gaia Text
Editorial director: Ferdinand Ranft
Chief editor: Marion Zorn
Cartography for the Road Atlas: © Mairs Geographischer Verlag
Design and layout: Thienhaus/Wippermann
Printed in Germany

CONTENTS

Discover Ibiza and Formentera!

Ibiza is synonymous with the good life, while on Formentera, rest and relaxation are the order of the day. Who could ask for a better combination?

Torrid nights, weird companions. Dancing drag queens in samba dresses gyrate in front of the disco called *Privilege*. Inside, the loudspeakers throb, and any number of lush blondes allow themselves to be groped by greying men in their forties covered with gold chains. Ibiza is an El Dorado for night folk, for Beautiful People, and for all those who want to be like them.

But it is also a Mecca for water sports enthusiasts, for fashion freaks, and, not least, for those in search of quietude. Ibiza is an island of superlatives. Here you will find the hottest discos, the most idyllic villages, the cleanest beaches, and the latest fashions. And that's not just the opinion of the Ibizans. The hundreds of thousands of spellbound tourists who swarm to the is-

land year after year to forget everyday life, for a few days or weeks think so, too.

Only a few kilometres from Ibiza, and recently made easily accessible by hydrofoil, lies Formentera, Ibiza's little neighbour, with its heavenly beaches and long stretches of deserted sand dunes. The island is a heaven for those seeking peace and quiet. Both islands, in earlier times called the Pitiusas, have something for every taste.

Since the early 1970s, Ibiza, which has a population of 75,000, has been one of the classic tourist destinations. The hippies of the 1960s — with flowers in their hair, the first Greens — were unwitting forerunners of mass tourism. While northern European travel agencies were developing Mallorca as a mass-tourism destination, the Flower Children from all over the world were discovering Ibiza, and making it their home.

The Flower Power movement took over the island

A view of Ibiza City from the harbour; in the background, the Upper City with the Cathedral and the castle

History at a glance

c. 1800 BC
Ibiza is mentioned in written sources

c. 650 BC
The necropolis at Puig des Molins is established

247 BC
Hannibal is said to have been born on one of Ibiza's neighbouring islands

123 BC
The Romans conquer the Balearics

70 BC
Ibiza is made part of the Roman Empire

AD 426
The Vandals occupy the Pitiusas; later the islands are ruled at various times by the Moors, the Franks, and the Normans

1114
Ibiza becomes a base for pirates of the western Mediterranean

1235
During the Reconquista, the Spanish recovery of Arab-occupied territory by Christian armies, troops of the Archbishop of Taragon in the service of Jaimes I take the islands and establish Christian rule

1469
The foundation of the modern Spanish state is established by the marriage of Isabella of Castille and Ferdinand of Aragon; the Pitiusas, which like the rest of the Balearics belong to the kingdom of Aragon, become part of the kingdom of Spain

16th to 18th century
Trade in the Mediterranean loses much of its importance after the discovery of America by Christopher Columbus in 1492

1936–39
The Spanish Civil War

1950
Tourism gradually begins to recover

1960
The Beautiful People of the 'Woodstock generation' turn the islands into Europe's Flower Power headquarters

1975
Franco dies in Madrid

1982
Spain joins NATO

1983
The Balearics become autonomous

1986
Spain becomes a member of the European Community

1992
Olympic Summer Games in Barcelona; World's Fair in Seville

1998
Hundreds of thousands of tourists enjoy themselves on Ibiza and Formentera

INTRODUCTION

by peaceful means, giving it its reputation as the Woodstock of Europe. Here, they gathered on the way from San Francisco to Katmandu: intellectuals, artists, and actors – they all met here. Ibiza made the headlines: sex, drugs, and wild parties with show-biz celebrities. The island became a favourite topic featured in the tabloids, which characterized it as the Rio of the Mediterranean, an image that the press has tried, with moderate success, to tone down since the early 1990s.

The inhabitants bear all this with near-stoic composure. This isn't the first time that strangers have made themselves at home on their island, taking it over for themselves. Though Phoenecians, Romans, and Moors have come and gone, the Ibizans and their culture have survived, into the post-modern era. The *Ibicencos*, as the 'real' inhabitants call themselves, are proud of their history and their culture, which can be traced back to the Bronze Age.

Although several museums testify to the turbulent past, such as the one in Ibiza City devoted to the Phoenician history, the best way to get to know the island is through its inhabitants. Their openness and tolerance are proverbial, and their ancient ways and customs have, especially in the rural north, withstood the pressure of progress.

In the hamlets around Sant Joan de Labritja, in Santa Agnès de Corona, and Sant Mateu d'Albarca, the clock seems to have stopped. Men

and women still wear traditional costumes, and not just to Sunday mass. Agriculture still contributes its fair share to the family income. In these areas, the island has been able to retain some of its original spirit. Not much has changed in the much-visited holiday resorts near Sant Miquel de Balansat, Portinatx, and Cala Sant Vicent, for example.

The southern part of the 'White Island', on the other hand, is a permanent carnival platform for stars and starlets – and, of course, for all those who wish to be like them. The rule here is: the crazier and wilder the costume, the better. Anyone seen strolling about in plain old shorts and a T-shirt can expect at best a pitying look, more often an outright disdainful glance.

Evenings in Sant Antoni de Portmany, the second-largest town on the island and its tourist centre, are just as eccentric. The only thing missing here is the flamboyance of Ibiza City.

Things are definitely quieter on the other side of the island, in Santa Eulària d'es Riu, which offers a clean beach and good tourist facilities, and has established itself as a desirable spot for those who are looking for somewhere to relax, not to be entertained. The place seems to be dead and deserted after 1 am. The only disco is hardly worth mentioning, and whoever wants another cool, refreshing cocktail when the hour is late needs to have some kind of vehicle at his disposal. On the other hand, there are some good restaurants here, and an exclusive yachting harbour, indications of the elevated tastes of the sort of visitor who chooses Santa Eulària d'es Riu as a holiday destination.

And those who find even Santa Eulària too exciting for those most precious days of the year have only to cross over to Formentera, Ibiza's small sister island of 4,000 inhabitants. Formentera is in the shape of a dumbbell, and is really only a southern extension of Ibiza. It is separated from the larger island by a mere 7-km stretch of water called the Els Freus. The tiny, unpopulated islands in the Els Freus go by the names of Ahorcados, Negres, Caracoles, Espalmador, and Espardell. The boat trip from Ibiza to Formentera takes about an hour, an hour which is well spent and not soon forgotten. Formentera is a paradise of endless beaches, broad expanses of sand dunes, and turquoise water. The unfrequented roads are a cyclist's dream (the network of bicycle paths is excellent). The highest point of the island, the plateau of La Mola to the east (192 m), affords ideal opportunities for enjoyable walks. You won't get lost on Formentera because the island is not big enough (95 sq km). Although the island is only 2 km wide at its narrowest point, and 20 km wide on its largest point, from the westernmost edge to the lighthouse at La Mola on the eastern end, it would still take you at least several weeks to get bored here. That is because there is a wide range of excursions possible and because the island offers interesting opportunities in the way of cultural attractions.

An exclusive holiday address: the Hacienda Na Xamena near Port de Sant Miquel

Although you can easily conquer Formentera by bicycle (it's only 16 km up to La Mola), it is really advisable to hire a car for a full tour of Ibiza, which covers 572 sq m and is one and a half times as large as the Isle of Wight. The island is 48 km long from Punta Grossa to Cap Llentrisca, and 24 km wide, from Cap Nonó to Punta Martinet. That makes it too large to cover in a day's cycling trip. But if you want to spend several days touring Ibiza by bike over, you will at least be spared the exertion of big hills. The only heights worth mentioning are in the south-west and the north-east. They are each interrupted by broad valleys and do not exceed 500 m.

The highest mountain, the Sa Talaia, in the south-west, near Sant Josep, is 476 m. The southern part of the island is particularly well suited to cyclists. Here, on the broad, level stretches near the salt works called Ses Salinas, there are practically no natural obstacles. Be adventurous, and leave the security of the inland for the coast. There, tucked away in the cliffs along the 165-km coastline, are what are called *calas* waiting to be discovered. Some of these little sandy bays, ideal for bathing, are also accessible by boat. So you don't really have to be the millionaire owner of one of those speedboats so common in Ibizan waters to play pirate for a day.

Brochures that describe local hiking trails have been available from the tourist-information centres here since 1992. So why not take advantage of them, grab your backpack, and tramp through fields and the broad olive and pine groves (the islands get their name, the Pitiusas, or Pine Islands, from these stands of evergreens), and experience for yourself the abundant, unique nature of this island world? The heady smell of the red-brown earth mingles with the scent of wild herbs, such as rosemary, thyme, and fennel. The display of flowers along the roadside will make your head swim — oleander, geranium, and hibiscus blossoms transform the landscape into a riot of magical colours, especially in the spring. The spiky fig-cactus is at first glance not quite as pleasant to look at, but it nevertheless fulfils an important sanitary function in the daily life of the Ibizans — its penetrating smell keeps the flies away from the outhouses of isolated *fincas* in the countryside.

Pre-eminent cultural historians have discerned traces of Neolithic influence from the Near East in the buildings of the *fincas* scattered across the islands. The plans for these simple yet functional farmhouses are never committed to paper. Rather, they have been passed down orally for hundreds of generations. Such great modern architects as Walter Gropius and the Catalan Josep Lluis Sert were much taken with these farmhouses. They saw some of their own theories applied in them, many of which are hundreds of years old. Since 1994, visitors have been able to catch a glimpse of the everyday life of the island's inhabitants, at Puig de Missa, in Santa Eulària d'es Riu, where a traditional *finca* has been turned into a fine museum of local history.

The climate of the Pitiusas is similar to that of the other Balearic Islands in that the sea exercises a direct and noticeable influence on the temperature, which rarely exceeds 30° C (86° F), even at the height of summer, and in winter rarely drops below 7° C (45° F). Most precipitation falls between mid-October and the end of March, almost always in the form of rain. Snow falls once in a hundred years in the Pitiusas. Bathing in the sea is possible from May on, when the sun has warmed the water sufficiently. Even though the climate is agreeable and mild, even in winter, most visitors used to come to the islands in the summertime. Only in the last few years the Pitiusas have begun to be a favourite winter destination. The exceptionally mild climate of these islands makes them an ideal place to spend the winter, especially for older people. They are an alternative to Mallorca, the largest of the Balearics.

The Ibizans welcome this latest development. They intend to give their island a new image that will also appeal to target groups that up to now have not been attracted to Ibiza or what it has to offer. The emphasis is now obviously on quality rather than quantity. It is hard to tell whether this new attitude is a reaction to the decline in the numbers of visitors that made itself felt at the beginning of the 1990s. At any rate, the planners

are convinced that the golden years of mass tourism are now over. New concepts and strategies are needed, since Spain is no longer the inexpensive holiday destination it used to be in the 1960s.

People who come to the Pitiusas now expect more than just sun and sand. Planners have recognized this fact and have decided in favour of exclusivity: golf courses and marinas are calculated to make the islands more attractive to visitors with larger purses. But the planners intend to make things here more attractive to the average tourist, to villages are being spruced up, the network of bicycle paths is being extended, and signposted hiking trails are being built. The *Plan de Embellecimiento* has already borne fruit: the beaches are cleaner and the small villages look better tended. Ever since drinking in the streets was made illegal and the mayor went on British television to say that rowdies were not wanted in his town even wild Sant Antonio de Portmany is not as wild as it once was. Ibiza is no longer interested in cut-rate tourism. Individuality in combination with quality — that's the way to appeal to the upper-middle classes.

The wickedly expensive superdiscos in the southern part of the island exemplify this trend. The former *KU,* in Sant Rafel, was for many years the leader among Ibizan discos. After several changes of ownership, this superdisco now operates under new management with a new name, *Privilege*, and is still a great hit on the Ibiza night scene. The competition is intense: others, including *Es Paradis* in Sant Antoni and *Amnesia* outside the Ibiza City, re-opened in 1992 after extensive renovation.

Ibiza ceased to be a secret among fans of the disco scene quite some time ago. The island has so much to offer in the way of music and dancing that it is difficult to beat. The larger dance floors, for example the *Pacha*, are so very exclusive that a mere mortal visitor (even after paying his entry fee of almost US $30) can be removed from his comfortable chair and relegated to a hard barstool because some minor pop star and his groupies have just invaded the place. Once they even cleared an entire hotel of paying guests to make room for Julio Iglesias and his entourage. (The guests were found alternative accommodation.) So be prepared for anything.

June is the month for fashion shows on Ibiza. 'Adlib', an abbreviation of the Latin *ad libitum* (which means 'as you like it'), is a style that evolved, with head-spinning speed, from the hippie fashions of the 1960s to the elegant, delightful, and breathtaking Ibiza fashions of the 1980s and 1990s. Unfortunately, only a few of the Adlib designers have their showrooms in town. Most of them live and work in old *fincas* in the countryside, and sell their wares in selected avant-garde boutiques in Ibiza City. One of the rare opportunities to enjoy the sight of these fashions all in one place

is the annual Adlib fair on the Vara de Rey. It is a spectacle without equal anywhere in the world.

Ibiza is frequently misrepresented, so don't be fooled by what people tell you. A good rule of thumb is, believe one-tenth of what you read and nothing of what you hear. Always see for yourself, even if you have to travel some distance to do so. It is true that Ibiza is no longer the 'Isla Blanca', the White Island, described by the Catalan author and painter Santiago Rusinol — even if a large number of Ibizans still turn out every spring to white-wash everything within reach, so that the place at least looks as it always has. But it would be far too easy to believe the 'real-life' tales of sex, drugs, and murder retold so often in the lurid weeklies. How else, one must ask, are newspapers sold? Not with true stories, that's for sure. Every visitor experiences Ibiza and its neighbouring island, Formentera, in a different way. For every unbelievable (and believable, for that matter) wild story in the tabloids, there is another about the peace and quiet that reign in this holiday resort. Remember, Ibiza and Formentera have something to offer every visitor. These islands, with their many and varied attractions, represent an ideal microcosm for all those who wish to undertake a journey of discovery. Of course, it is lots of fun to read the newspapers, but do try to keep an open mind and discover for yourself the variety and charm of the Pitiusas!

11

Trendsetting fashion, folk music, and quiet beaches

Variety is the keyword on Ibiza and Formentera;
you'll find all the essentials here

Abel Matutes

No one else has exercised so much influence and power over Ibiza as the banker-politician Abel Matutes Juan — The Godfather, as the tabloids often call him. About 2,000 people work for him on Ibiza alone, in hotels, banks, and other enterprises. Nothing goes forward on this island without his approval. Hardly anyone else has done so much to stamp his own image on the face of present-day Ibiza. Matutes, the scion of a long-established Ibizan family, is an old hand at the business of mass tourism. He transformed Ibiza into a holiday destination in the 1970s, when he was vice president of the Fomento de Turismo Ibiza. Since 1990, when a crisis in the tourist trade was first openly discussed, Abel Matutes has once again made himself

The mild climate and luxurious plant life of the Pitiusas delight visitors at any time of year

heard. It was he who suggested a complete turnaround in the leisure and holiday trade by targeting different groups. It's obvious that people have been listening to his ideas. Those who own business relating to the tourist industry on Ibiza are now even putting those ideas into action. Hotels are being equipped with central heating and double-glazing for the winter trade, marinas are springing up like mushrooms, and a whole new series of golf courses is planned that will soon attract the more affluent vacationers from northern Europe and overseas to the Pitiusas.

Adlib

Adlib, an abbreviation for the Latin *ad libitum*, stands for Made-on-Ibiza fashions. Another meaning of the phrase is, 'As You Like It'. A group of designers working on the island came together in the 1970s with the slogan 'Wear What You Like' to develop the highly imaginative and fantastic hippie gear so frequent here into their own sort of style, which took off very quickly. What began as a revolt against traditional fashion, a liberation from styles imposed from above, was quickly taken over by the Establishment. Designers of the Adlib group make no mass-produced items, only exclusive creations that no hippie could possibly afford. Nevertheless, Adlib promotes itself as a mould-breaker, a movement that goes against the current and flies in the face of traditional fashion. Adlib causes year after a year a sensation, with its ever-more liberal and body-hugging designs, and is especially successful in June, when the company holds its annual three-day fashion event. Big names, such as Elena Deudero, Arruda, Melania Piris, and Laura Victoria, display their latest collections at this event.

Alcohol

It has long been commonplace in casual conversation to complain about the cost of basic necessities having risen considerably in Spain over the past several years. Alcohol is still an exception to this trend. But this is not the only reason for the popularity on Ibiza of wine and brandy and the local liqueurs, all of which go down at lunch and dinner as smoothly as café con leche at breakfast. It's simply because the drink is good here. The Spanish wines and brandies are excellent, and can stand comparision with the better varieties of France any day.

One local speciality is the herbal liqueurs, the *hierbas*, distilled on the island. They are especially to be recommended after meals here, which are often made with more olive oil than one is accustomed to. Restaurants frequently offer their guests a free sample of this liqueur after dinner. But watch out — the effect of alcoholic drinks strikes with double force under the hot Mediterranean sun.

Ibiza's extensive beaches offer plenty of room for volleyball and other sports

14

Beaches

Many holidaymakers see nothing but sun, sea, and sand during their two- or three-week vacations. Ibiza's most-visited tourist attractions are not its museums, or its ancient ruins (although there are some), but its beaches. You will find detailed descriptions of the more important beaches in every town.

Catalan

This is what might happen: you arrive on Ibiza, hire a car, take your guidebook, a couple of years old, in hand, and start off on your explorations of the island. But after the first few kilometres you realize that you are in a strange new world, with traffic signs that you can't read or find in your guidebook. What has gone wrong? What's happened is, all the place names on the road signs on Ibiza and Formentera are now in Catalan, which has become the officially recognized language of the islands. The older guidebooks supply only the Spanish versions of the names. To head off such surprises, all place names in this Marco Polo guide are given in Catalan, so that a journey of discovery does not turn into a comedy of errors.

Discos

Whoever is turned on by wild disco music can turn night into day on Ibiza. This scene is not for lovers of harmonious melodies, it's more for cool yuppie types with thick wallets. And age counts for little, for the men at any rate. The disco scene doesn't really get going here until around 2 am. Although there's a full complement of dance floors on the island that would leave any big European city gasping with admiration, there are really only two or three unbeatable spots. The *Pacha* in Ibiza City and the *Privilege* (formerly *KU*) in Sant Rafel are the leaders among the luxury discos, followed by *Es Paradis* in Sant Antoni and *Amnesia*, outside Ibiza City. *Space*, on the Platja d'en Bossa, which opens only towards morning, is always worth a visit. Every celebrity spends at least one night here. Roman Polanski, Niki Lauda, Julio Iglesias, and even stars from among the current Top Ten of rock enjoy being seen prancing about in the big discos. Only these demigods can afford more than one night in these super-palaces of dance. Ordinary mortals, on the other hand, who have to pay up at the entrance and again at the bar (a cocktail costs around US $12) are pushed to their financial limits.

Drugs

The days have long gone when solemn hippies casually passed reefers among themselves in drowsy comradeship. The thing now is *extasis*, a chemical stimulant taken in pill form that apparently enables one to dance entire nights away without stopping. And it's no longer the hippies who do the dealing, as in the 1960s. Today, mafia-like gangs control the drug trade.

The environment

It is not surprising that most of the damage to the environment of a holiday island such as Ibiza is the result of mass tourism.

The building of blocks of vacation flats and hotels without official permission, the dumping of low-grade sewage directly into the sea, and remorseless extinction of entire species of fish by snorkellers and divers armed with spear-guns, are only some examples of environmental abuses that point to the ever-more-urgent need for legal measures to be taken to maintain and protect the ecology of the Pitiusas. But it is early days yet. In spite of all these abuses, however, the natural environment is still in fairly good shape. Several beaches, such as those at Santa Eulària d'es Riu and at Cala Tarida, have several times been awarded the European Union's Blue Pennant for cleanliness and good hygienic conditions. Other winners of the Blue Pennant are pleasure-boat marinas, such as Ibiza Nueva and Marina Botafoch. Planners are now working to ensure that more communities receive this award. They believe that so far hygienic standards on the Pitiusas are so high that in fact every beach could be awarded the Blue Pen.

Families
For most of the Spanish, and the Ibizans are no exception, life without one's extended family would not be half the fun. They enjoy nothing so much as Sunday-evening dinner with the entire family, a regularly-enacted ritual. The more relatives and friends, the better. Northern European individualism and intimate groups are unknown here. This is certainly not to everyone's liking, but is surely an advantage if you want to take your children along on holiday. It is not unusual to see toddlers or even infants in the streets or in restaurants as late as midnight. Everyone here is ready to help with children, and when you want to go out by yourselves, you will have no trouble finding a place to park the kids. Hotel staff and private agencies will gladly help you locate a dependable babysitter.

Fauna
The Phoenicians came to Ibiza to establish burial sites. According to their beliefs, the earth of a cemetery must be free of venomous beasts. Even the dead, or so the Phoenicians thought, can suffer from the bites of poisonous spiders and scorpions. It is a fact that there are no poisonous creatures on the Pitiusas, which can be a great comfort to the living, and especially to anyone who wants to hike here. All the same, you should take care, when picnicking in a clearing in the pine forest, that you do not pitch your blanket on one of the numerous anthills. And don't be alarmed if, just when you've found a comfortable place to rest, you hear a sudden rustling in the undergrowth. It will be only one of the shy local lizards, *Lacerta Pityusensis*, in its glittering brown-green, iridescent skin, which exists in about 30 varieties. They are quite harmless. However, you should keep an eye out for the Pharaoh dogs, the *Podenco Ibicenco*, which Cleopatra is said to have used while hunting on these islands. Yet, this breed has become so rare in recent years that most of them are domesticated and are

generally to be seen at the end of a lead. If you want to see something of the aquatic life of the Mediterranean, you don't necessarily have to go scubadiving or snorkelling now that the Delphinarium, near Platja d'en Bossa, is open. The broad and little-frequented beaches of Formentera were in earlier times the breeding-ground of giant sea-turtles, which have been known to weigh in at 500 kg. They have since been driven off by a burgeoning tourist industry.

Fincas

These old farmhouses, unlikely as it may seem at first, are among the most exclusive forms of accommodation in the Pitiusas. The really 'in' people don't live in luxury flats along the beach, but instead in these old rural properties that one sees scattered here and there across the countryside. Often, they are accessible only by four-wheel-drive vehicles. They have been restored to the last detail and fitted out with all the latest modern conveniences. People gladly pay the often outrageous prices for a night's lodging in one of these houses. What makes the *fincas* so attractive is their novelty and their location. While they give the occupant near-perfect peace and quiet, tucked away deep in the folds of the countryside as they are, they are often only minutes by car away from the best discos and some of the most exclusive restaurants in the Mediterranean.

Flora

Early summer is the best time for those who want to experience Ibiza and Formentera in all their verdant glory. It is in early summer that the brilliant colours of the almond and pomegranate trees offset the reddish-brown earth tones of the Pitiusas. But it is in September, and again in December, that almost all plant life is in full bloom. Beach lilies and amaryllis are two of the late bloomers among the local flora. If you fancy olives in your aperitif and have always wanted to see the millennia-old trees on which they grow, you might consider an excursion to the northern part of the island. Here, near Sant Miquel de Balansat, for example, there are still extensive olive groves. You will, however, look in vain for large vineyards here. The bitter-sour *vino pagés* is still produced only in limited quantities. Winemaking is not very profitable on the Pitiusas, and what is made is for local consumption, not for export. But, you can get a glass of the Ibizan wine, if you want, in most of the village pubs.

Folk music

People who are familiar with Spanish folk music say that the Ibizan musical tradition is one of the liveliest in Spain, perhaps outdone in this respect only by the Andalusian flamenco tradition. There are groups here and there throughout the islands that perform the old folk music and dances, and that give regular performances during the summer months. The best-known of these groups is that from Sant Miquel de Balansat, whose weekly performances in front of the local church allows visitors to experience Ibizan culture first-hand. Whomever would like to take some music home with them will find a wide assortment of Ibizan folk music in the record shops in Ibiza City. Unfortunately, the instruments of this traditional music — for example the *xeremia* (a flute) or the *espasi* (a sort of triangle) — are to be had not in the shops but only through personal contact with the folkloric groups.

Hippy markets

Ibiza is an El Dorado for people who love attractive jetsam. There are weekly hippy markets all over the island. The largest and best-known of these is the one on the grounds of the country club at Es Caná. But be warned: it might take some time and patience to find a rare item or work of art among the merchants' itinerant wares. Don't hesitate to talk to the vendors. You might be able to find out some interesting things by doing so, such as how the items are painstakingly made by hand, the Arab leather masks for example, or the tuned wind chimes. Communication is not a problem here. Most of the artisans are, like you, from somewhere else, not from the island. And once you get to know the dealers (only some of whom are still recognizably hippies), you can start negotiating over price.

Paella

This ever-so-typical Spanish rice dish originally came from Valencia, the country's principal rice-growing province. Paella is so widespread and is made in so many variations that every Spaniard and everyone who knows the country will, if you ask for the recipe, tell you a different way of making it. And every one of them will assure you in fervent tones that his or her way of making the national dish is the one and only original method. But these experts will all agree that among the ingredients that go into the big round paella pan have to be saffron rice, meat, fish, chicken, and shellfish (mussels, crab, etc.). Paella pans come in all imaginable sizes. These days, the dish is served up on individual plates, but in former times people simply helped themselves to the common pot. Since paella has to be made fresh, and is cooked immediately before eating, portions must usually be ordered for two or more people.

Sa Penya

This former Bohemian quarter of Ibiza City, once so romantic with its narrow alleys, on the harbour beneath the Dalt Vila, the Old Town, grows seedier and more dangerous every year. One top-notch boutique after another has gone under in the Carrer de Mare de Deu, once one of the principal shopping thoroughfares in Ibiza City. Now, the drug-dealers openly carry on real gang wars in the streets of Sa Penya. During these disagreements it can happen that one clan will set fire to the house of another, with its members in it. This doesn't mean that you will risk life and limb by strolling through the narrow byways of this quarter. But, do be careful, and take along only the smallest amount of money.

18

Ses Salines

The salt flats of Ibiza and Formentera, Ses Salines, are among the most important natural habitats of plant and animal life in Europe. They were declared a European natural reserve in 1992. The protected area is about 35 hectares in extent, and, over the years, has often been threatened by plans to build hotels. Conservationists have taken up the cudgels in defense of these areas and are hoping that this ecosystem, unique in several respects, can be preserved for future generations by making it part of the European network of nature preserves.

Sun

No matter how often one warns those who repair to southern climes for their holidays not to overdo it on the first day under the strong ultraviolet rays of the sun, it always happens. The pale faces from the north are transformed after one day on the beach into swollen redskins, with serious burns covering their bodies. It also pays to take precautions when touring the island on a moped wearing only shorts and a T-shirt.

Tourism

The tourist trade has certainly changed the face of these islands. However, if you hike through the near-deserted fields of the north, you will come across remote *fincas* where the farmers still bring in the harvest with horse-drawn waggons. In these places you can still get a taste of the old, uncomplicated life of traditional Ibiza. In the cafés and restaurants of the holiday resorts, on the other hand, you will have the impression that you have never left home. It is comfortable in these places, the sun is warm, and the atmosphere relaxing. If you try out your Spanish when ordering something, you will not meet with any great success. The waiter, equipped with well-trained eyes and ears, will have spotted you as an Anglo-Saxon and will from that moment on answer only in his fluent English, whether you produce your bits of night-school Spanish or not. The island has completely oriented itself towards tourism, and lives almost exclusively from tourism. In fact, Ibiza has become dependent on tourism. When people in the Pitiusas speak of a crisis in the tourist trade, they are speaking of a general economic crisis. The economy of these islands would not survive without the holidaymakers. That is why the authorities here have worked out alternative strategies for the tourist trade. The Ibizans are now determined to put quality before quantity. Hotels have been modernized, the golf course at Roca Llisa has been expanded (three more courses are at the planning stage), and the number of moorings for pleasure boats has doubled, all of this quite recently. Things do indeed seem to be looking up. In 1994, for the first time in years, there was a noticeable increase in the number of visitors. nant if the communities concerned applied for it. Cleanliness is in the wind here.

The 'Moustache' has the best fish

Discover Ibizan specialities, served up with Spanish flair and savoir vivre

The view across the clear blue sea is one thing, the enticing aroma that rises from the plate before you is another. *Arroz a la marinera* is simply delicious. Prepared over an open fire, it is something you get only at *El Bigote* (The Moustache), in Cala Mastella. The pleasure one derives from this dish is something that has to be experienced to be believed. But, many holidaymakers pass up the opportunity to try it or anything else local for that matter. The average tourist is usually interested only in familiar, plain cooking along the lines of steak or chicken, with chips and salad, or is even content with a hamburger at Mc-Donald's. Above all, insists the typical tourist, no fancy foreign fare. Stick with what you know. It is all too often overlooked, that Catalan and Ibizan cuisine is absolutely superb. Who among us has tasted *guisat de peix*, a delicately-flavoured sort

In Sa Capella de Can Basora, a temple of the culinary arts near Sant Antoni, one can find excellent fish specialities

of bouillabaise, or *sopa i bullit*, a hearty soup with lamb and vegetables? Convinced? So now you want to try them? No problem. There are plenty of restaurants on the island. But a word of caution: the kitchen doesn't always have everything that is listed on the menu. But with a little patience and luck you will find here, like anywhere else, the proverbial exception to the rule. Whoever knows his or her way around can find a restaurant that serves up *burrida de ratjada* and *sofrit pagés,* even along the waterfront of Ibiza City's harbour.

Restaurants in rural areas are a special treat on the Pitiusas. They are often located in *fincas* that are hundreds of years old. The addresses of these exclusive establishments are often a secret to be passed on by those who know of them. Unfortunately, these restaurants are often accessible only by car, but it's well worth the trip. A dinner in a *finca* can be an unforgettable experience.

Table matters

Try living according to the Spanish principle of *ocio*, the fa-

The Spanish cuisine can be an enlightening experience in many of the fincas, old farmhouses in the countryside

bulous tradition of *dolce far niente*, or of doing nothing at all. It's wonderful, at least while you are on holiday. Take your time over meals and enjoy the lively entertainment afforded by a local restaurant as you wait for the next course. Don't look at your watch all the time or ask the waiter why the cook needs a whole half-hour to whip up your eight-minute steak. Start these leisurely habits with breakfast, and happily fritter away the time with one or two oven-warm *ensaimadas*, yeasty rolls baked in lard, with a *café con leche*. Why not, indeed? The morning is long, and lunch anywhere in Spain, including the Pitiusas, doesn't make an appearance before 1 pm. (The midday meal is generally available in restaurants between 1.30 and 3 pm.)

Naturally, a siesta of two or three hours is called for after lunch. You really should adopt this old Spanish custom, particularly since life practically comes to a standstill between 2 and 5 pm. The shops are closed, and there is hardly anyone to be seen in the streets. An air-mattress for the beach, or a sofa indoors, will come in handy at this point.

People eat dinner very late here. While it is true that most restaurants open for dinner at around 8 pm, they don't really get going until after 10. It's only past midnight that you will get dinner everywhere without problems. The evening meal takes even longer than lunch. It often begins with an aperitif in a nearby bar and ends with a *cubata* in an outdoor café. Like the midday meal, dinner usually consists of three basic courses. The *entrada* is often a mixed salad *(ensalada mixta)* or a soup *(sopa)*. A Spanish speciality that is served only during the hot summer months is *gazpacho*, a cold vegetable soup made of tomatoes, garlic, onions, and peppers. If you want to eat Ibizan-style, order the hearty stew called *sopa i bullit*, which consists of mutton, bone-marrow, bacon, and vegetables. After that, there is either a meat or a fish course. The Ibizan specialities here are a fish soup called *guisat de peix*, ray in almond sauce *(burrida de ratjada)*, and a farmer's stew made of braised lamb and pork, chicken, peppers, potatoes, and garlic, called *sofrit pagés*. Or you can order a paella. Saffron rice, mussels and other seafood, various sorts of meat, and peppers and onions are the classic ingredients of this typical Spanish dish.

For dessert, try a *greixonera* (a sort of pudding made of *ensaimadas*), *macarrones de San Juan* (macaroni cooked in sugar and milk and sprinkled with cinnamon and lemon juice), or a *flam* (a pudding with a caramelized sauce).

Drink

You must leave the towns and go into the countryside to sample the *vino pagés*, the Ibizan local wine. The farmers make this wine only for their own consumption, and it is hardly ever exported. One drinks other things in the bars and restaurants of Ibiza, although the local wine can be found in small cafés frequented by Ibizans. Wine from the Spanish mainland is what you will find in the majority of restaurants and *bodegas*, especially wine from the Rioja region, where viniculture is a speciality. Examples of Rioja are *Marqués de Cáceres, Faustino I*, and *Federico Paterna*. Another region, Navarre, offers *Señorío de Sarria* and the Penedés, a superior variety that stands up well to comparison with well-known and much dearer French vintages. The restaurants serve wine in full bottles, half-bottles, and carafes. If you place importance on quality, you should look out for the classification *Denominación de Origen* on the label. Particularly good wines bear the appellation *Gran Reserva*. In the event that the unaccustomed oil and garlic in the food lie uncomfortably in your stomach after dinner, order an Ibizan herbal liqueur *(hierbas)* at the end of the meal, or one of the many good Spanish brandies. If you prefer a non-alcoholic drink, and especially if it is a hot day, try a *horchata*, a refreshing concoction of *chufas* (Brazilnuts), ice-water, and lemons. The strong and delicious coffee comes in three varieties: *solo* (black and very strong), *cortado* (with a bit of milk), and *con leche* (with a lot of milk). This last, *con leche*, is the breakfast favourite.

Hippy markets, pullovers, and leather goods

Ultra-tight, scanty tangas are ever-popular gifts for those you left at home

Super short miniskirts, transparent blouses, and racy garments of leather and cloth are identifying features of the Adlib style, which put Ibiza on the fashion map, and which many people still consider a fashion trendsetter. Every year, in the spring, the Adlib group organizes its great fashion event, where the latest creations of the local desigers are displayed. The things that are shown here in the spring, and sold in the boutiques of Ibiza over the summer, are the summer fashions of northern Europe for the following year — the organizers at least are convinced that it works that way. The commercial centre of Ibizan style is Ibiza City. Here, in the harbour area, you see one boutique after another lining the streets. Given the variety of the items on offer,

it is often extremely difficult to distinguish quality goods from junk. But one should be clear about one thing: the clothes sold here bear these high prices not because of the quality of the material they're made of. What count here (and add to the cost) are, above all else, the label and the unusual design. If you're looking for high quality, you've simply come to the wrong place. But if you're looking for far-out, body-hugging designer gear, and are prepared to lay out the equivalent of between US $250 and US $500 for it, then this is the place for you. There is no doubt about it: the clothes sold in Ibiza's boutiques are refreshingly novel, not the usual sort of thing you get back home in the High Street, and are a lot of fun — when money is no object. If you have to keep an eye on your finances and you are still interested in Ibizan styles, you will have no choice but to wait for the annual end-of-season sale in October.

Any lover of fashion should definitely stop in at Paula's in Sa Penya, the old fishermen's quarter of Ibiza City

25

The leading boutiques then clear their racks with reductions of up to 60 per cent. If you would like to see the designers at work, you will probably be disappointed. The Ibizan designers have retired to the countryside, where they live in their *fincas*, most of which are extremely difficult to find.

As Adlib was in the process of becoming fashionable, a group of exclusive art galleries began a series of exhibitions on the island that has since become famous. These shows confirmed Ibiza's reputation as a Mecca for intellectuals and artists. Works by such well-known European painters as Eduard Micus, Erwin Bechthold, Heinz Mack, Will Faber, and Hans Hinterreiter, all of whom lived and worked on the island, part of the year at least, were shown for the first time here. In the early 1970s, hundreds of lesser-known artists began to arrive on Ibiza and Formentera. They hoped to find here a sufficiently large market for their works. There then arose what are still today misleadingly called the 'hippy markets'. People gathered at these markets during the summer months to sell their handmade items to the hordes of tourists who invaded the island during the season. These markets, most of them weekly events, are still being held, but the hippies are these days less in evidence. The hippies were replaced as they faded out of existence by professional vendors, who were able to make some extra money by selling their wares at these markets. All that is left of these original hippy markets is the name and a few romantic memories. One of your very few opportunities to see the artists at work on Ibiza is in Sant Rafel de Forca. This little village has in the past few decades made a name for itself, and not only among the disco fans. Here, on the road between Ibiza City and Sant Antoni de Portmany, you can visit a whole series of one-person workshops that produce handmade ceramics according to ancient Punic designs. On Formentera, you might stop to examine the display of local handicrafts at La Mola, on the eastern side of the island. Especially attractive are the sweaters knitted from Formentera wool. Spain was for decades known as a country where one could find leather goods at particularly low prices. Those days are, however, long gone. If you want to buy trousers, jackets, or other leatherware, these days you'll have to pay almost as much on the Pitiusas as you would at home. On the other hand, the items here often come in extravagant designs that are worth the price. That of course goes for other leather items made on Ibiza as well such as handbags, shoes, and belts, which are of a high enough quality to stand comparison with the products that are produced in the big cities. Those items are mostly brand-name goods, the sort that command high prices all over the world.

Along with leather goods, alcohol and tobacco are classic gifts from the Iberian Peninsula for the people back home. Spanish wines, Spanish sparkling wine (made according to the

Some of the pottery on Ibiza is modelled on ancient Punic designs

same method as French champagne), liqueurs, and brandies are available in the Ibizan *bodegas* and supermarkets at much lower prices than in shops back home. The wines of the Rioja region are especially recommendable. The sparkling wines, particularly those of the Penedés region, such as *Codorniu,* are also excellent. There are liqueurs for every taste (Ibizan liqueurs and herbal bitters are called *hierbas* and *palo*). There are good brandies, one brand called *103,* is especially fine, and even better when the bottle bears the Black Label, the *Etiqueta Negra*. Even a simpler brandy, such as the one called *Magno* (from the *Osborne* distillery), titillates the palate, and is definitely more reasonably priced. If you want to try something more exclusive, even extravagant, sample the *Cardenal Mendoza,* a truly excellent brandy from Jerez de la Frontera *(Hermanos Sanchez Romate).* Its subtle caramel taste has won it many fans who drink little else,

and who will shell out an astonishing US $5 in the shops at home for this *coñac*.

Cigars and cigarettes are not only imported into Spain, but also manufactured there. Connoisseurs are of the opinion that the quality of the tobacco from the Canary Islands *(tabaco negro)* is excellent. But the Virginia blends of Spain are, according to those who have not yet given up this addiction, not to be sneered at. Recommended brands are *Fortuna* and *Ducados,* although this last may be a little strong for northern European and North American tastes.

In general, the shops are open from *9 am–1.30 pm and 5 pm– 8 pm, Mon–Fri, and 9 am–2 pm, Sat.* Although most businesses are closed on Sunday, many shops and boutiques, especially in the tourist areas, are open all day on weekends. Opening hours have been regulated only since 1994, and shop owners don't observe the official times very strictly.

Public festivals and pilgrimages

The festive high points on the islands are between May and October

PUBLIC HOLIDAYS

1 January *Año Nuevo* (New Year)
6 January *Reyes Magos* (Epiphany)
1 May *Día del Trabajo* (Labour Day)
25 July *Santiago* (St James)
15 August *Asunción* (Assumption)
12 October *Día de la Hispanidad* (Columbus Day)
1 November *Todos los Santos* (All Saints' Day)
6 December *Día de la Constitución* (Constitution Day)
8 December *Inmaculada Concepción* (The Feast of the Immaculate Conception)
25 December *Navidad* (Christmas)
26 December *San Esteban* (St Stephen)

The movable feasts are:
March/April *Jueves Santo, Viernes Santo* (Maundy Thursday, Good Friday)
May/June *Corpus Christi* (Corpus Christi)

Ibiza's rich musical heritage has been preserved by those who love traditional music

FESTIVALS

In Catholic Spain, the local saints' days take on a special meaning in the festival calendars of many parishes. And, on Ibiza and Formentera communities celebrate the name day of their local saints with parades and pilgrimages as well.

17 January *Sant Antoni de Portmany*
21 January *Santa Agnès*
12 February *Santa Eulària d'es Riu*
19 March *Sant Josep de sa Talaia*
23 April *Sant Jordi de ses Salines*
30 May *Sant Ferràn de ses Roques* (Formentera)
24 June *Sant Joan de Labritja*
16 July *Es Cubells*
8 September *Jesús*
16 November *Santa Gertrudis de Fruitera*
12 December *Nuestra Señora del Pilar, El Pilar de sa Mola* (Formentera)

FESTIVALS & LOCAL EVENTS

February/March
Festival de Primavera
On the Pitiusas, the religious events calendar begins with this

spring festival in honour of Santa Eulària d'es Riu. Various cultural events are held outdoors over several weeks, weather-permitting. More detailed information about specific programmes, etc., can be obtained from the tourist information bureaus.

Holy Week
Semana Santa

The Santa Semana, Holy Week, is in these islands, as everywhere in Spain, the most important and most significant week in the religious calendar. *Cofradias*, or religious brotherhoods, on the Pitiusas as elsewhere in Spain, organize daily parades through the streets of larger villages, processions that reach their climax on Good Friday. Men in long black penitents' robes and hoods that remind one of the Ku Klux Klan bear the crucified Christ through the streets, an occasion that the Catalan singer Joan Manuel Serrat has so movingly described in the Saeta Antonio Machados. Whatever one's own religious background, it is hard to remain unmoved whilst watching this spectacle.

1 May
Día del Trabajo

The first of May is a national holiday in Spain, as almost everywhere else. On this day, the inhabitants of eastern Ibiza hold in Santa Eulària d'es Riu a gigantic festival with street processions.

June
Semana de la Moda

★ Adlib Fashion Week in Ibiza City, organized by a group of designers living on Ibiza, is held under the patronage of Princess Smilya Milyanovich, still active in spite of her advanced years. She never ceases to beat the drum for Ibiza's designers and their styles. During Fashion Week, which has now been going for more than 20 years, the members of the Adlib group display their new creations as part of a series of fashion shows.

July
Music festivals

There are ★ music festivals on Ibiza every year, in July, for every taste, including those who like less-jarring melodies. Special favourites are the national jazz festival and the International Festival of Classical Music. The concerts, always well-attended, are sometimes held outside, in front of the spectacular backdrop of Ibiza City's Dalt Vila, or Upper City.

5 August
Nuestra Señora de las Nieves

★ The festival of Our Lady of the Snows is observed over several days every August. This festival, which celebrates the construction of the Cathedral in 1235, comes to a climax on the evening of 5 August with a gigantic fireworks display over the Dalt Vila in Ibiza City.

24 August
San Bartolomé

The largest public festival in the town of Sant Antoni is held during the week of 24 August, when the people celebrate the name day of St Bartholomew. This tourist town in the western part of the island celebrates the day with great enthusiasm, and throws in everything a Spanish festival should have. Young and old alike turn out for this unforgettable experi-ence. The main attractions are the *verbena*, a fair popular with all, and a spectacular fireworks display.

October
Semana Internacional del Cine

Just to make sure that visitors do not get bored at the end of the season, the cinemas on Ibiza organize an international film week every year, in October. While the programme is not exactly newsworthy, this is one's only chance on Ibiza to see films that rise above the level of the latest Rambo saga. The *Cine Serra* in Ibiza City *(Passeig de Vara de Rey)*, the *Cine España* in Santa Eulària d'es Riu *(C/ San Jaume)* and the *Cine Torres* in Sant Antoni de Portmany *(C/ Obispo Torres)* do show foreign films during the summer months, including some in English, French, and German, but not particularly good ones. During the International Film Week, though, one can see films by François Truffaut, Martin Scorsese, Wim Wenders, and other well-known directors. The tourist information office on Ibiza has programme information for the Festival.

The sun and moped excursions

The beautiful weather here is perfect for excursions, and the moped is an ideal way to travel round these islands. But if you sling a leg over one of these machines, clad only in shorts and a T-shirt, and spend the whole day spinning over these well-built roads without a break, in order to get the most out of the rental fee, you will pay a heavy price the next day, at the latest. Swollen flesh, second-degree burns, and a throbbing head will make it clear that precautions should be taken during the first few days under the scorching Mediterranean sun.

Wild abandon and joie de vivre

Ibiza City is a carnival in the summertime –
colourful, youthful, and full of surprises

Bronzed gigolos dripping with gold chains, leaning casually against their Porsches, beautiful young women in skimpy bikinis throwing come-hither glances right and left, garish costumes, and wild celebrations night after night – that's Ibiza City in the summer, a frenzied carnival, colourful, youthful, and always

The statue of General Varas de Rey, the island's most famous son, in the centre of Ibiza City

full of surprises. It's quite a different story, though, in Santa Eulària d'es Riu and Port de Sant Miquel. Anyone who expects the wild nightlife of the capital in those places is surely doomed to disappointment. And anyone who has booked a hotel room in Figueretes or Platja d'en Bossa has to remove himself to the centre of activity, the harbour district of Ibiza City, to enjoy the inviting glances and the nightly show put on by the Party People. Every year, from June to Sep-

---

Hotel and restaurant prices

Hotels
Category 1: over 8,000 pesetas
Category 2: 3,000-8,000 pesetas
Category 3: up to 3,000 pesetas
These prices are for one person in a double room (excluding breakfast).

Restaurants
Category 1: over 5,000 pesetas
Category 2: 3,000-5,000 pesetas
Category 3: up to 3,000 pesetas
These prices are for an evening meal including a starter, a main course, and dessert, plus drinks.

Important Abbreviations

C/.	Carrer (street)	**Pl.**	Plaça (square)
Av.	Avinguda (avenue)	**s/n**	sin número (no house no.)

tember, tens of thousands flock here to witness the spectacle that they have heard or read so much about. Yet, only a few play an active role in the goings-on; most are there as spectators. Here, in what was once the capital of the European hippy movement, one encounters a curious mixture of completely different types with only one thing in common: they want, each in his or her own way, to be a part of this summer carnival that has made the name Ibiza a synonym for wild abandon, creativity, joie de vivre, and scandal. Nowhere else in Europe can one give such free rein to one's imagination, nowhere else is the line between reality and fantasy so thin as on this giant summer stage.

Holiday resorts have sprung up outside the capital; in Ibiza City itself there are only a few of these large hotel complexes. To the east is Platja Talamanca, to the south Es Vivé, Figueretes, and Platja d'en Bossa, all of which have grown so much that they now border on Ibiza City. But anyone who knows his or her way around here and has a few special addresses, stays away from the big package-deal hotel blocks and finds other accommodation, either in Ibiza City itself or in one of the quieter and not so built-up places outside town. Alternatives are near Santa Gertrudis de Fruitera, Sant Rafel de Forca, or directly on Ses Salines, near La Canal.

MARCO POLO SELECTION: IBIZA CITY & ENVIRONS

1 Amnesia
One of the most spectacular discos on the island (page 46)

2 Cantonada
The best Ibiza-style fashions, all in lace (page 42)

3 Galería Carl van der Voort
The art scene's Number One address (page 42)

4 Platja de Ses Salines
The most beautiful beach in the southern part of the island (page 45)

5 Museu d'Art Contemporani
You'll find striking examples of modern art here (page 38)

6 Museu Arqueològic del Puig des Molins
This museum takes one back into the Ibizan past with its collection of Punic artefacts (page 38)

7 Pacha
A stunningly successful discotheque, where the action starts at 2 am (page 47)

8 Privilege
The former *KU* has new owners, a different name, and renewed success (page 47)

9 The potteries in Sant Rafel
Here you may purchase hand-thrown ceramics of the highest quality (page 49)

IBIZA CITY

☛ City Map inside back cover

(106/A-B3) Whoever comes to this centre of stars and starlets, of freaks and intellectuals, of hippies and homosexuals, should begin getting their bearings by learning the three most important quarters: Dalt Vila, Sa Penya, and La Marina. Dalt Vila is the Upper City, where the Cathedral overlooks the city from the top of the hill. Sa Penya is the former fishermen's quarter direct on the harbour, and La Marina is the New Town west of the San Salvador church, going towards Passeig de Vara de Rey (formerly Paseo Vara de Rey). Most of the 25,000 inhabitants of the town live in La Marina. The city is at its most lively in Sa Penya, the place where it all began, several thousands of years ago. It was here that the first settlers on Ibiza built their dwellings, near where the Estacio Maritima is today.

These days, because fewer and fewer tourists make their way up to the district above the Calle Mayor, the area is becoming ever shabbier. Boutiques and bars keep closing their doors there. The crowds now go to the quay below, and push through the narrow lanes in that area in their quest for entertainment. There is now one exclusive boutique after another in the Calle Mayor (the new Catalan name of which, Carrer d'Emnig, has been slow to catch on), and in the nearby side-streets. The surprising thing is, though, that most of the designers belonging to the Adlib group do not have their own shops here, but rather sell their creations through other shops on a commission basis. The selection is wide and always-changing. The big hit of one year can flop the next. The exclusive shops, that is those along the Calle Mayor quite near the quay, often change hands. Exceptions are the near-classic names, such as *Elena Deudero*, *Paula's*, *Cantonada*, and *Salambo*. The Carrer de Mare de Deu, once so important to shoppers, has lost its attraction to the big names in fashion since drug-related crime got out of hand there. But there is still an exceptionally lively bar scene. In Carrer Garijo and the Andenes del Puerto, parallel to the waterfront (Passeig des Moll), you will find the capital's best-known restaurants and cocktail bars. But it is true that business has visibly gone downhill in this area, ever since some of the biggest names migrated to the Marina Botafoch.

In Botafoch, on the other side of the harbour, there is now a new 'Miracle Strip', not so overrun or as frantically busy as the Harbour Mile of Sa Penya, but more tasteful and exclusive. All the big names are in evidence here. The big discos have their own cafés, there is a branch of the famous *Mary Sol* and one of the café *Bolero*, where celebrities gather. The Marina is the stars' watering hole of the 1990s. Even if you don't show up in your own speed-boat, this place is worth a visit.

SIGHTS

Dalt Vila **(U/D-E3)**
The Dalt Vila, or Upper City, of Ibiza City was renovated at

great expense in the early 1990s and is now hardly recognizable. There are no traces of the old collapsing city walls, or of the filthy alleyways that used to characterize the place. For a good view of the harbour district, walk through the Portal de ses Taules and the old fortifications, up to the ⚐ city walls.

Monument to the Corsairs   (U/E2)

The sole monument to the Corsairs in the entire Mediterranean stands on the quay in Ibiza City, close to where the big Mallorca passenger boats dock. The 'Monument a los Corsarios' well befits the island and its inhabitants, who in the course of their history were never shy about taking advantage of unorthodox means to stand up for their rights. And so it was in the early years of the 19th century, when they engaged the Corsair Antonio Riquer Arabi to carry out retribution raids against pirates who had made things extremely difficult for trade all around the Mediterranean. Arabi chalked up his greatest victory in 1809, when his ship sank the vastly superior English brig *Felicity* in Ibiza Harbour. As a token of thanks for this heroic deed, the Ibizans erected an obelisk to Arabi and his crew on the very spot from which they had breathlessly watched the battle for an entire day. Arabi went on to forge a legitimate career, like so many pirates, and was made a officer in the Spanish Navy for his skill, his valiant deeds, and his services to a grateful nation.

Nuestra Senora de las Nieves   (U/E3)

⚐ The Cathedral of Ibiza City is consecrated to Our Lady of the Snows, the patron of the 'White Island'. She reigns high over the city, in the centre of the Dalt Vila, and is the symbol of the Upper City. The walls of this imposing Cathedral are integrated into the medieval fortifications, the Castillo, and are a reminder of the city's turbulent past. The various and changing rulers of the island built their temples and mosques on this spot before the foundations of the present Cathedral had been laid, at the end of the Spanish Reconquista. Construction ended as late as 1592, when the sacristy, which now houses the diocesan museum, was finished. If you are interested in centuries'-old vaulted ceilings, retables, and monstrances, you shouldn't miss the little museum in the Cathedral. If not, it is also a rewarding experience to save the entry fee and instead rest on one of the wooden benches to quietly absorb the refreshing peace and quiet of this house of God. Across from the Cathedral is the Casa de la Curia-Sala de Exposiciones del Museo Arqueológico, the former bishop's palace. *Open 10 am–1 pm daily and (except Sat and Sun) 3 pm–6 pm; admission 500 pesetas. Pl. de la Catedral, Dalt Vila, mass 10.30 am Sun*

Vara de Rey   (U/D2-3)

His grateful countrymen dedicated an entire promenade to 'The Hero of Cuba', General Vara de Rey (1840-1898). His larger-than-life figure brandishes his rapier in a threatening gesture and thus recalls Spain's struggle to hold on to Cuba, its last American colony. It was clear even before the decisive battle took place, in 1898, that the little army that Ibiza's most famous son led into the field against the *Nordamericanos* was defending an utterly hopeless position. Although Vara de Rey and his men fought valiantly, they lost the battle — as was to be expected — and with it Spain's last hold on the New World. The general himself was killed in the fighting. Ibiza City's most

Dalt Vila, the Upper City of Ibiza City with the Cathedral of Our Lady of the Snows and the Castle

important boulevard, the Passeig de Vara de Rey, bears his name to this day.

MUSEUMS

Museu Arqueològic d'Eivissa   (U/E-F3)

Particularly worth seeing in this museum are the items recovered from graves at Ca Na Costa, on Formentera. These objects proved for the first time, in the 1970s, that the Pitiusas were inhabited in prehistoric times. Other items on display provide information on the Punic and Roman settlements up to the era of Islamic occupation and the Reconquista. Just one visit to the museum will give you a good overview of more than 3,500 years of Ibizan history. The museum buildings themselves, as well as the exhibits, warrant a visit. The museum was founded in 1907, and was then accommodated in rooms belonging to the old university and the Capilla del Salvador. During extensive renovation work in the 1980s, it was enlarged, and extended to the medieval fortifications. The Baluarte de Santa Tecla has since been connected to the main rooms of the museum by an underground tunnel, which takes the visitor like a time machine into vanished worlds. This extraordinary museum is well worth a visit. *Open 10 am–1 pm and 4–7 pm daily except Sun; Pl. de la Catedral; admission 500 pesetas*

Museu Arqueològic del Puig des Molins   (U/C4)

★ The items displayed in this museum are the remains of Car-thaginian, or Punic, civilization on the Pitiusas. Hundreds of artefacts are exhibited on two storeys of the building and have made the museum the repository of the world's most important collection of objects relating to the history of Carthage. Most of the pieces here come from one of the more than 3,000 burial chambers of the necropolis at Puig des Molins. There are four tours per day through this Punic cemetery, during which visitors can descend to the underworld through one of the narrow shafts that cut through this City of the Dead. It is clear from the holes in the partition walls separating the individual graves that some of them have been plundered by graverobbers. This work of destruction was stopped only at the beginning of the 20th century, when an organized excavation of the necropolis was undertaken. The museum, founded in 1966, was reopened after extensive renovation in 1981. A good guidebook to the museum is available in several languages and costs only 50 pesetas. *Open daily 10 am–1 pm (except Sun) and 4–7 pm; Via Romana, 31; admission 500 pesetas*

Museu d'Art Contemporani   (U/E3)

★ Even if you don't usually go to museums, because you find them too dusty and boring, and because most of them display only works of established artists, you should pay a visit to the Museum of Modern Art, near the Portal de ses Taules. Its two vaulted exhibition rooms are part of the centuries'-old Castle of Ibiza. There's nothing old here and more than things of only historic interest. In these rooms you can admire the works of artists who in the late 1960s made Ibiza known throughout the world. The collection consists of almost 400 works by painters from Japan, France, Austria, Germany, Britain, and Belgium. Different temporary exhibitions are organized from time to time, each with a separate theme, using these works. Masterworks by Eduard Micus, Will Faber, and Hans Hinterreiter belong to the permanent collection. Works such as *Superding I* by Erwin Bechthold, which so outraged the culture and art establishments in the 1970s, now arouse at the most a wan smile. Or is it that the picture's misleading subtitle (sin titulo = Untitled) was no accident after all? *Open daily 10 am–1.30 pm and 5 pm–8 pm (except Sun); Dalt Vila (above the Portal de ses Taules); admission 500 pesetas*

RESTAURANTS

Ama Lur (106/B3)

This splendid country restaurant is, unfortunately, reachable only by car. But it is well worth the trip. There are only a very few restaurants on the island where you can dine in such elegance and intimacy as here, although it must be said that this atmosphere has its price. But the excellent Basque cooking will make up for that. This cuisine from the other side of Spain has been perfected here at *Ama Lur.* Only a few minutes

from the city centre by car, the *Ama Lur* is an ideal place to go when you want something better than the usual run of restaurants. Open daily 8 pm to midnight; *Carretera Ciutat Eivissa-Sant Miquel, km 2.3; Tel. 971 31 45 54; category 1*

Bahía (U/E-F2)

Juanito, the owner of this small restaurant on the Miracle Mile of Ibiza City, is unique, as are his daughter and his son, who help out as waiters. The speciality of the house is roast chicken. Although Casa Juanito, as the *Bahía* is called by regulars, is in the lower price range of Ibizan restaurants, it is still one of the favourite haunts of the disco-going jet-set, because of its location. *Open daily 7 pm–midnight; C/. Garijo, 1; Tel. 971 31 10 19; category 3*

Beach Club Guarana (104/E5)

✅ A good restaurant, directly on the Platja de ses Salines. A beautiful terrace affords wonderful views of the ocean. Here you can get absolutely delicious paellas, *fideuas*, and every other sort of fish dish. Meals are served down on the beach, too. What more could you ask for? *Open daily 10 am–2 am; Tel. 971 39 54 44; category 2*

Sa Caldera (U/B3)

Very few tourists are seen in this restaurant, since it is in the newer district of the city, where the local people live. That means that you get good value for your money. That *Sa Caldera* is patronized mainly by Spaniards speaks well for it. The service is especially good here. *Open daily*

*7 pm–midnight, C/. Bisbe Huix, 19;
Tel. 971 30 64 16; category 2*

C'an Alfredo (U/D2-3)

❧ This restaurant has been here
since the end of the 1930s, so
you can be sure that you haven't
fallen into a tourist trap. On the
contrary: *C'an Alfredo* has been a
solid hit with the Ibizans for
years, and features a magnificent
menu. This is one of the restaurants where you can try and enjoy the traditional Ibizan cuisine.
*Open daily (except Mon and holi-
days) 10 am–midnight; Passeig de
Vara de Rey, 16; Tel. 971 31 12 74;
category 2*

Cap des Falco (105/E5)

Although this restaurant is
situated at the salt works, Ses
Salinas, opposite the airport, one
does not hear the noise of planes
landing and taking off. It offers
a splendid fishing-village backdrop and a good look at the
jet-set, who find this a conve-
nient meeting-place. Especially
to be recommended is the fresh
oven-baked fish. Don't forget
to book; this place is popular.
*Daily 12.30 pm–3 pm and 7 pm–
midnight; Ses Salines; Tel.
608 63 64 72 (mobile); category 3*

El Cigarral (U/C2)

Family-run restaurant with delicious grilled meat and fish
dishes. Here you will find the
most extensive wine list on
Ibiza. *Open daily 1 pm–4 pm and
7 pm–midnight; C/. Fray Vicente
Nicolás, 9; Tel. 971 31 12 46; category 1*

El Divino (U/A5)

An excellent restaurant with superb food. You'll find everything
here from bream with mashed
potatoes to steamed filets Saint
Pierre in a butter sauce. This restaurant on the harbour has the
best of everything, including
prices. All this and a pretty terrace, too, where VIPs come to
celebrate in style. *Open daily
9 pm–6 am; Passeig Marítim; Tel.
971 19 01 77; category 1*

El Faro (U/F2)

◁▷ Exquisite cuisine at the Ibiza
City lighthouse, with a shady
terrace and a good view of
the sea. You'll find very good
paella here, and *fideuas*. If you are
prepared to pay for it, you can
enjoy the lobster, fresh oysters,
and other very tempting fish
dishes. *Open daily 11 am–2 am;
Pl. de sa Riba, 1; Tel./Fax 971 31
32 33; category 1*

El Olivo (U/E3)

By far the best restaurant
on the Plaça de la Vila, directly behind the Portal de ses
Taules. *Open daily 7 pm-midnight;
Pl. de la Vila / C/. Luis Tur i
Palau, 7–9; Tel. 971 30 06 80; category 1*

Los Pasajeros (U/D3)

� The restaurant can be found
in a little sidestreet, above a café
that is a haunt of the ex-hippies,
the Alternative People, drop-
outs, and all those who choose to
swim against the current. The
crush is impressive. The queue
often leads down to the street,
and people put up with it, even-
tually to claim one of the cov-
eted seats. Guests don't get their
own tables here. You share with
other people, which encourages
communication. This place is always worth a visit because of its

congenial atmosphere, even if the menu is nothing to write home about. *Open daily 8 pm– 2.30 am; C/. Vicent Soler, 6; category 3*

San Juan   (U/E-F2)

Here is one of the very few restaurants in Ibiza City where the food is as good as it is inexpensive and simple. The atmosphere is unpretentious, there is no hint of the smug or self-satisfied. The stars and starlets come here to eat. Those who know the local scene value this place as a clean and reasonably priced restaurant with classic Spanish cooking. If you've eaten here once, you'll put up with the longish wait for a table again. At any rate, you won't be disappointed. *Open daily 1.30 pm– 3.30 pm and 6.30 pm–11 pm; C/. Guillem de Montrí, 8; Tel. 971 31 07 66; category 3*

San Telmo   (U/E2)

A French restaurant in the harbour district of Ibiza City. When other restaurant-owners are wringing their hands at the lack of customers, Ycon Pamart is wondering where to put extra tables to accommodate the rush of his hungry patrons. The most popular house specialities are tender steaks and paper-thin French crêpes for dessert. Foreigners who live on the island in particular have flocked here for years. The restaurant is situated in a cul-de-sac a little out of the way, but can be found nevertheless. Highly recommended. *Open daily 7.30 pm– 1 am; Sa Drassana, 6; Tel. 971 31 09 22; category 2*

El Sausalito   (U/F2)

The prices are almost scandalous, but *El Sausalito* is all the more exclusive for that. An absolute must for voyeurs – for almost two decades celebrities have been gathering here to be spoiled by French chef Alain Mion and to be stared at by the ordinary diners. Be sure to show up before 8 pm, or even better, reserve a table. You will otherwise find nowhere to sit in *El Sausalito*, at least not during the high season. *Open daily 8 pm– midnight; Pl. de sa Riba, 5/6 (at the end of the quay); Tel. 971 31 01 66; category 1*

Teatro Pereira   (U/E-F2)

This French restaurant, most elegant and decked out in great style, is in the first storey of the former theatre. The *Teatro Pereira* is the regular meeting-place of many of the resident foreigners because of its extraordinarily good food and its cosmopolitan atmosphere. *Open daily 1 pm– 3 pm and 7 pm–midnight; C/.Abel Matutes, s/n; Tel. 971 39 05 81; category 2*

Victoria   (U/D2)

Spanish home-cooking has absolutely nothing to do with the northern European variety. This restaurant is where you can confirm this piece of wisdom. This is where you will be served dishes that are so prized among the locals. *Open daily 1 pm–3 pm and 8 pm–11 pm; C/. Riambau, 1; no Tel.; category 3*

SHOPPING

Many people spend their entire holiday rummaging among

the latest rags in the Ibizan boutiques. Ibiza is known for its far-out styles, even when one can't wear these things anywhere but on the island. What is sexy, distinctive, and much in demand here, can cost you your job back home, or bring on a summons from the police for outraging public decency. But, if you look around a bit, you can find clothes here that are somewhat 'alternative' and that can be safely worn in London, New York, or Toronto. While on the boutique circuit, don't forget to take a look at the street markets, which are open only before noon, and the small traditional shops that have, no one quite knows how, managed to survive the onslaught of mass tourism.

Organic Shop Natural   (U/D2-3)
If you don't plan to give up your biodynamic-nutrition principles during your holiday, you will find everything you need in this shop. *C/. Miquel Caietà Soler, s/n*

Cafés Ibiza   (U/E2)
Foreign coffee-lovers as well as locals will no doubt find their preferred blend in this shop, just across from the fruit-and-vegetable market. *Pl. de la Constitució, 14*

Calzados la Balear   (U/E2)
There is every imaginable variation of the *alpargatas*, the classic Spanish rope-soled shoe, in this little shop, and much else besides. *C/. de sa Xeringa, 11*

Calzados Sansano   (U/C3)
If you still dream now and then of the days when leather shoes

were exceptionally inexpensive in Spain, you should pay a visit to this shop, even if it is a little off the beaten path. *C/. Aragó/ C/. Bisbe Huix*

Cantonada   (U/D2)
★ Exclusive fashions by Teresa Bermejo, all in white lace. *Av. Comte de Rosselló, 10*

Desigual   (U/E2)
One of the few Ibiza boutiques that have become classics. The *Desigual* trademark has for more than a decade stood for youthful leisure fashions. *C/. Barcelona, 5*

Dom   (U/E2)
Things of glass and porcelain, unique gift items, and other bric-a-brac. *C/. de sa Creu, 7*

Elena Deudero   (U/B2-3)
Leather fashions showing African influence, sometimes in bright colours. Certainly not for a formal dinner-party and not cheap either. *Av. Isidor Macabich, 17*

Farrutx   (U/D2)
Fashionable shoes, handbags, belts, and leather clothing. *Av. Bartolomeu de Rosselló, 12*

Francisco Prats   (U/E2)
Artistically-thrown and original ceramics. *C/. de sa Creu, 13*

Galería Carl van der Voort   (U/E3)
★ The name has taken on the near-mythological sound of times gone by. After some difficult years, during which the best-known gallery on Ibiza was open only at irregular intervals, it now looks as though the art scene has got its second wind.

The gallery is 'in' again. *Pl. de la Vila, 13*

Galería Lanz (U/E3)
Whoever has a weakness for pottery will love this place. Here you may purchase original ceramic work modelled on modern and classic designs. *Pl. de la Vila, 17*

Hamacas (U/D3)
This original shop for hammocks has the best selection of Spanish, Mexican, and Brazilian types in all Spain. They are also right for your balcony back home, or the back garden. A real paradise for all lovers of the siesta. Prices from US $60. *C/. Vicent Cuervo, 11*

Herbolería (U/E2)
The decades seem to have passed by this traditional shop in the Lower City without leaving a trace. Catalina Colom still sells her home-blended medicinal herbs and spices here, in little paper bags. Many of her herbs are cheaper than what you would pay back home. Take a deep breath in this shop, and come away enchanted. *C/. de sa Creu, 25*

Librería Vara de Rey (U/D2-3)
Following a dispute over who had the rights to the concession for the big newspaper kiosk on Passeig de Vara de Rey opposite the *Montesol*, the business had to close down. Its role was taken over by the bookshop further up the hill, where you will readily find a good selection of Spanish and foreign newspapers and magazines. *Passeig de Vara de Rey, 22*

Magic (U/D2-3)
The most magical thing here are the prices. Despite this, however, you will find the latest Adlib fashions. The focus is on shoes and other leather goods. *Passeig de Vara de Rey, s/n (next to Café Montesol)*

Mango (U/D2)
A fashion house arranged along supermarket lines. In spite of the not-exactly-inspired designs, *Mango* is popular, especially with the younger crowd. *C/. Riambau, s/n*

Markets (U/E2 and A-B3)
❖ Ibiza City has three markets, all of which remain open until noon. The public fruit and vegetable market is along the sides of the marketplace on the Plaça de la Constitució, the Mercat Vell. Just around the corner, toward the city wall, is the fish market, in a covered hall. The Mercat Nou, where you will find meat, fish, fruit, and vegetables, is also a covered market, between the C/. Extremadura and the C/. Canarias, directly adjacent to the bus station in Av. Isidor Macabich. Shopping here gives you an idea of what the old Ibiza was like.

El Moham (U/E2)
Attractive junk, ceramics, and books. *Pl. de la Vila*

Pastelería Los Andenes (U/E2)
The always freshly baked *ensaimadas* have been for sale here every day for years. Many visitors take one of the giant pastries home with them as a sweet souvenir. *Andenes del Puerto, 3*

The peace and quiet of the Upper City of Ibiza City is in direct contrast to the busy life of the harbour district

Paula's (U/E-F2)

Armin Heinemann, a former architect from Cologne, has made a real hit out of his little fashion shop. People often queue up in front of the window to goggle at the most original creations on the island within. A thick rope across the door ensures that only genuinely interested customers get in. *C/. de Mare de Déu, 4*

Pepa Bonett (U/D-E2)

Seductive materials are transformed into clothing in all colours of the rainbow. Here are fashions in genuine Adlib style, guaranteed to have been designed and tailored on Ibiza. *C/. de sa Creu, 4*

Salambó (U/E2)

Cristina Buscetto can show you in her boutique what happens when Italian style meets Ibizan creativity. *C/. Josep Verdera, 4*

The End (U/D-E2)

While this is one of the largest boutiques on the island, it produces no designs of its own. Instead, the big names of the fashion world are represented here with their latest models. The attractive saleswoman will show you what these styles look like on a shapely and modish body. But beware: if you give way to your acquisitive desires here, a visit to *The End* could mean the end of your holiday budget. *C/. de sa Creu, 26*

ACCOMMODATION

Club Med Ibiza   **(U/A5-6)**
This exclusive holiday resort is at the far end of the Platja d'en Bossa. There is a programme of organized activities here, a rare thing on the Pitiusas. This place is not for those in search of peace and quiet, however, since it is near the airport. *Platja d'en Bossa; 420 rooms; Tel. 971 39 67 84, Fax 971 39 67 59; category 1*

El Corsario   **(U/E3)**
One of the best addresses in Ibiza. Famous show-business personalities often stopped over here in the 1950s. *C/. Poniente, 5, Dalt Vila; 14 rooms; Tel. 971 30 12 48, Fax 971 39 19 53; e-mail: elcorsario@ctv.es, category 2*

Las Nieves   **(U/D3)**
A simple but clean guest house in a quiet street parallel to the Passeig de Vara de Rey. *C/. Juan de Austria, 18; 50 rooms; Tel. 971 31 58 22; category 3*

El Palacio   **(U/E3)**
An eccentric sort of hotel with a magnificent view of the harbour. The suites are decorated with reminders of famous Hollywood stars. The Marilyn Suite, in pink, is something to write home about. *C/. de la Conquista, 2; Tel. 971 30 14 78, Fax 971 39 15 81; e-mail: etienne@ctv.es, category 1*

Royal Plaza   **(U/C1)**
When this hotel, once the only four-star hotel in Ibiza City, was reopened in 1981, few believed it had much of a future. Today, this house has earned a secure place in the hotel sector of the island's economy. *C/. Pere Francès; 117 rooms; Tel. 971 31 00 00, Fax 971 31 40 95; e-mail: royalpla@xpress.es; category 1*

La Torre del Canónigo   **(U/E3)**
◁▷ A beautiful hotel in a carefully restored 14th-century cloister. Situated at the highest point of the Dalt Vila, it offers a splendid view and all modern comforts. Luxury apartments and studios with terrace and swimmingpool. *C/.Bisbe Torres, 8, Dalt Vila; 9 rooms; Tel. 971 30 78 43, Fax 971 30 38 84; category 1*

Ventana   **(U/E3)**
Why not reserve a room with balcony and a view of the harbour area? All rooms are equipped with satellite television, a bath, a telephone, and a minibar. *C/. de sa Carroça, 13; Dalt Vila; 13 rooms; Tel. 971 39 08 57, Fax 971 39 01 45; category 1*

SPORTS & LEISURE

Ibiza City doesn't offer a beach for bathing. People who want to swim go either to Platja d'en Bossa, known as Rolex Beach, or a bit farther on, to Ses Salinas, where one can choose between the Platja d'es Cavallet, which is one of the official nudist beaches, and the ★ Platja de ses Salines, a long, sandy beach. It is, unfortunately, rather crowded, especially on weekends. But there is, at the Platja d'en Bossa, a big aquatic amusement park with water chutes and several swimming pools. Although the admission prices (between 750 and 1,500 pesetas) are quite steep, a visit is well worth your while, especially with children in tow. They will be enchanted with the place. Horse-lovers meet at the Sunday trotting races at the Hipódromo de Ibiza, on the road that leads to the airport. Racing times are published in whole-page advertisements in the local newspapers. Although there is a bullfight arena, a Plaza De Toros, in Ibiza City, there have not been any bullfights here for years. The bulls are so expensive that they are no longer to be seen grazing in Ibizan meadows. Whoever cannot resist this typical and bloody Spanish sport must travel to Valencia, Barcelona, Madrid, or Seville.

ENTERTAINMENT

Amnesia   (106/A2)
★ A few kilometres outside Ibiza City, on the road to Sant Antoni, is the famous disco called *Amnesia*. This discotheque, which belongs to the island's classic dance-palaces, has had a turbulent past. *Amnesia* was reopened in 1992 after extensive renovation. *Carretera Sant Antoni, km 5; admission 4,000 pesetas*

Café Sydney   (U/A5)
Expensive convertibles and racy motorcycles. This café, situated at the lower end of the new marina is a favourite gathering-spot of the rich and famous and the mobile-phone demi-monde. From 5 pm on, it's nonstop Harley-Davidsons, Porsches, and beautiful girls. *Passeig Marítim, s/n*

Casino de Ibiza   (U/A5)
Not only can you play roulette, blackjack (vingt-et-un), baccarat, and chemin de fer, but there are also shows with in-

The evening spirit settles over Ibiza City — the night owls crouch in the starting-blocks

ternationally renowned stars. If you want to gamble, don't forget to bring your passport or other identification. *Passeig Marítim, s/n*

Keeper (U/A5)
A disco and bar in the immediate vicinity of the Marina Botafoch. Meeting-place of all those who want to be 'in'. Open from 10 pm on. *Passeig Marítim, s/n*

Malibu (105/E5)
A beachside bar with a view of expensive Rolex watches, muscular male bodies, a lot of yachts, and pretty women. *Platja de ses Salines*

Mar y Sol (U/D-E2)
This is the place where, after dinner, over coffee or a nice pick-me-up, one decides who goes to which disco with whom. *Passeig des Moll, s/n*

Montesol (U/D3-4)
The *Montesol* is not only the oldest hotel on Ibiza, but a café rich in tradition as well. *Passeig de Vara de Rey*

Pacha (U/E2)
★ The *Pacha* is the king and queen of all discos on Ibiza. Whether the music is much better than in the others is arguable, but it is much more attractively packaged here. The light and sound effects, including a smoke machine, are well worth seeing and hearing. The latest trend among the insiders is first to look in at *km 5* (say: kilómetro cinco; *Carretera Ciutat Eivissa-Sant Josep, km 5*) and then, from 2 am, to go on to *Pacha* to dance on through the rest

of the night. *Av. 8 de Agosto, 27; admission 5,000 pesetas*

Privilege (105/F2)
★ A spectaclar super-disco in Sant Rafel de Forca between Ibiza City and Sant Antoni. The former *KU* is under new management and has a new name. It has once again become the favourite gathering-place of film stars, race-car drivers, and millionaires. *Sant Rafel; admission 4,000 pesetas*

Space (U/A5)
This is the disco on the Platja d'en Bossa for tireless night owls. *Space* opens at 7 am, when the other establishments close. One of the most far-out joints on the island. *Platja d'en Bossa; admission (includes a drink) 2,000 pesetas*

Teatro (U/E-F3)
One of the 'in' bars in the back of the former Calle de la Virgen. If you want to experience a completely different world, you'll be welcome here. *C/. de Mare de Déu, s/n*

Teatro Pereira – La Cantina (U/E-F2)
These days, there is Tex-Mex food without garlic, and a crazy band to listen to, in the converted and extensively rebuilt *Teatro Pereira. C/. P. Sala, s/n*

INFORMATION

Oficina de Información y Turismo (U/D3)
Open daily 9.30 am–1.30 pm and 5 pm–6.30 pm Mon-Fri; Tel. 971 30 19 00; Passeig de Vara de Rey, 13 bajo

The police show no mercy to parking violatiors

Nimbly, and using old rusted-out jeeps as tow trucks, the Policía Municipal cruise the narrow byways of the inner city of Ibiza City well into the early hours of the morning in their eternal quest for parking violator. The police in Ibiza seem to have stopped handing out parking tickets entirely. Their motto now is, Tow It Away! To save yourself the trouble and the money, park outside the centre of town.

SURROUNDING AREA

La Canal   (105/E-F5)
La Canal, the salt port of Ibiza, is only 9 km south of Ibiza City, and is connected to the capital by a regular bus service. Here are two of the most beautiful beaches of the entire island: Es Cavallet and Ses Salines. If you're lucky, you can see them loading in the nearby salt works, where the salt is produced by means of evaporation. You get a free sample of this product of nature (in a salt-shaker) when you eat in ❖ *Mar y Sal*, which has been serving outstanding Spanish cooking for more than 20 years (*category 2*). The restaurant is a guest house as well, where you can stay overnight if you book early enough (*9 rooms; Tel. 971 30 74 42; category 3*). Mar y Sal is not a large place, and not particularly luxurious, but very comfortable. It is also situated in a very beautiful spot.

Figueretes   (106/A3)
This suburb is about 2 km from the centre of Ibiza City. This area consists largely of what were once modern hotel and apartment blocks. Most of these buildings were erected some 20 years ago, and only very few

have been renovated since, so one mustn't expect great comfort or luxury in this district. The beach here consists of only a small strip of fairly dirty sand, so that most visitors sunbathe at the nearby Platja d'en Bossa, even if it is several minutes away on foot.

The *Gallo de Oro* is a pleasant restaurant in Figueretes *(C/. Galicia, 15; Tel. 971 30 60 03; category 2)*, which features as one of its specialities Indonesian fare. The younger crowd meets in *Mississippi*, the 'in' bar of Figueretes, to enjoy loud music. *C/. Pais Vasco, 12*

Santa Gertrudis   (102/A-B5)
This village is a secret among those who know the island well, and a meeting-place for the resident rich and famous. It is a smallish place, but nevertheless there is a lot going on. Even though Santa Gertrudis is little more than a handful of houses gathered round a simple church, a lively cultural scene has come to life here. There is, for example, the *Galería Punto A (Tel. 971 31 74 25)*, which organizes regular exhibitions of the works of Ibizan painters. This is no small matter for the island's artists. If they can get their work shown

here, they will be taken seriously by the public and also by experts. Anyone who is interested in Ibizan antiques will find a worthwhile selection in the *Galería del Elefante (Tel. 971 31 35 81; closed Tue)*. Residents and locals meet in the Bar Costa *(Tel. 971 19 70 21)*, where about 40 hams hang drying from the ceiling among the paintings of South American artists. It may be this bizarre aspect of the decorative scheme that has contributed to the success of this establishment, which appeals to residents of the island and visitors alike. And the paintings are really worth seeing.

The attractions of Santa Gertrudis are rounded off by two excellent restaurants, the *Plaza (Tel. 971 19 70 75, category 2)* and the newer *Le Jardin de Santa Gertrudis (no Tel.; category 3)*. One can eat quite well in both these restaurants, which offer a very comfortable atmosphere.

Sant Rafel de Forca   (106/A2)

A visit to this little place on the expressway between Ibiza City and Sant Antoni is really worth the trouble, especially if you are interested in ★ Ibizan ceramics. Many artists, particularly those who make replicas of ancient Punic designs, have their workshops here. You can find single pieces guaranteed to have been made by hand on Ibiza, at extraordinarily reasonable prices. The workshops are easy to find since they are all on the road to Sant Antoni. If you think you might be interested in this handiwork, it's best to rent a car for the drive.

And if you are more interested in the culinary arts, you might be tempted to pay a visit to the restaurant here called ❧ *El Elefante (Tel. 971 19 80 56; category 1)*. Although the French proprietors took over the place only recently, it already looks as though they will be able to carry on the tradition, complete with excellent reputation, of the former *Grill San Rafael*. There is a lot to enjoy here, not only the good French cooking, but also the view of the Dalt Vila in the distance. Nowhere else in this area can you eat as well as here, in such pleasant surroundings. It's still an insiders' secret, but the *Indiana Café* has a sort of Far West atmosphere and is at the same time rather posh. The food is Mexican-inspired, the portions are generous, and the prices quite reasonable. *(Can Botas; Tel. 971 31 14 64; category 2)*.

In the spirit of Marco Polo

Marco Polo was the first true world traveller. He travelled with peaceful intentions forging links between the East and the West. His aim was to discover the world, and explore different cultures and environments without changing or disrupting them. He is an excellent role model for the travellers of today and the future. Wherever we travel we should show respect for other peoples and the natural world.

Idyllic beaches and turquoise water

Lovely little coves, tranquil landscapes – the countryside around Sant Antoni delights with its unique brand of charm

The pine trees sway slowly back and forth in the mild morning breeze, and the waves fall gently on the rocks. The first swimmers splash through the turquoise water, while other early risers stretch out their pale bodies on the warm sand to enjoy the sun. The Cala Salada will be full of people in a few hours, under their beach umbrellas stuck in rows in the sand. Even so, the bay will not have lost all its attraction. It is one of the many sandy coves tucked in among the cliffs in the southwestern part of the island that do not suffer at all in comparison with those of the northern coast. The Cala d'Hort, for example, is one of the more beautiful bathing beaches on the entire island. From its sands, one has not only an unbeatable view of the magical twin islands Es

Blue water and fine sand at the beach in the Cala d'Hort – there are idyllic coves for swimming like this all over the west coast

Vedrá and Vedranell, but as well one can sample the daily catch in excellent fish restaurants. The western part of the island offers a host of alternatives to simply relaxing on the beach. If you're on the lookout for a worthwhile souvenir, or want something sensible and practical to take back to those who stayed at home, there is always the possibility, when you've explored the shops of Sant Antoni, of a brief swing by Sant Josep de sa Talaia. It's a small place, but very pleasant. The authorities have clearly put a lot of money into the town's amenities in the last few years. There are now wide pavements that invite one to take a leisurely stroll past the old, highly atmospheric bars. The Sa Talaia, at 476 m the highest point in the Pitiusas, is another occasion for a walk, or hike. You'll find the beginning of the path up the hill just behind the bar called Bernat Vinya in the centre of Sant Josep. In the event that you are not in a hiking mood, but want to see something of the island's interior anyway, choose an overcast day to take the small train that goes to Santa Agnès, a tiny village only a few km north of the vast tourist hotels – but part of a completely different world. And who knows, you might let yourself be talked into a short hike to another village, Sant Mateu, six km east of Santa Agnès.

SANT ANTONI

(**101/D6**) The waves slap rhythmically against the quay. The fishing boats swing back and forth under the warm rays of the morning sun. Ropes creak gently, the gulls shriek. The port is still all but deserted. Only a couple of fishermen are to be seen, cleaning and mending their nets on the quay. The Passeig de Ses Fonts is dead to the world. The bars and restaurants are still closed, the only passers-by are the street-cleaners wielding their brooms. Most of the people who will come out to populate the streets and beaches of Sant Antoni in another two or three hours, are still immersed in their peaceful slumbers. But not for too long, since soon enough the metal shutters of the shops will be rolled up, waiters will set the tables in the restaurants, and the merchants will put up their displays. And around noon, music – House, Hip-Hop, and Heavy Metal – will begin to boom from the loudspeakers of the saloons. Soon the first thirsty customers will come to take their places at the bar.

In some ways a fishing village, in others a setting for big hotels – nowhere else on Ibiza is the contrast so striking as in Sant Antoni de Portmany. It is clear to see, externally, that tourism has altered what was once a fishers' port. To what extent, can be seen from the skyline along the coast. Great hotel blocks and tall blocks of flats tower over the beaches, and here and there one finds the concrete shell of a hotel that was never finished, for lack of money – mute witnesses to a too-fast and badly planned building boom. Almost 90 hotels and pensions with about 12,000 beds, more than 70 apartment complexes with a total of almost 2,000 large and small holiday flats, more than 100 restaurants, a dozen discotheques, and countless bars – that is the tourist infrastructure of Sant Antoni. A big city? No, not at all. Only 7,600 people live here. If you count the surrounding communities of Sant Rafel, Santa Agnès, und Sant Mateu, the total still barely comes to 14,000. But in the high season, the number of inhabitants swells enormously. During these months, the place known to the Romans as *Portus Magnus* and a few hundred years later to the Arabs as *Portumany* is one of the most popular holiday destinations on the island. The reasons are, of course, the idyllic bathing coves, clean beaches, good food, and the night life to be found in the 'West End' of Sant Antoni, the entertainment quarter between the Carrer Ample and the Carrer del Mar. Comparison of the night life of Sant Antoni with the 'scene' in Ibiza City is laughable, but enough goes on here to provide fun until dawn. And most certainly at a better price than in the big city. Young people in particular travelling on tight budgets find Sant Antoni's nightlife worth recommending.

SIGHTS

Fortified churches

The fortified church here, built in the 14th century, stands amid the new buildings of the recently developed part of town. The inhabitants of Sant Antoni built it a little away from the harbour on a slight elevation, in order to better defend themselves against the marauding pirates so common in those days. Its upper parts, like most of the other fortified churches of Ibiza, was originally equipped with cannons, well into the 19th century. This house of God is dedicated to Saint Anthony the Eremit (hermit), also called Saint Anthony of Egypt, who lived in the third and fourth centuries. *Pl. de sa Esglèsia*

RESTAURANTS

Sa Capella de Can Basora

★ It's worth it to fast for a week, then blow the money you've saved on one fantastic meal in this unusual restaurant. Sa Capella de Can Basora is decorated to resemble a country house. It is built within existing walls that have stood here for 300 years. The building was originally planned as a chapel but was never finished. Finally, at the end of the 1970s, it was converted into this restaurant. Wonderful Ibizan and Spanish specialties in mediaeval atmosphere, with classical music. *Open daily 7.30 pm– 1 am; Carretera Sant Antoni–Santa Agnès, km 0.5; Tel. 971 34 00 57; category 1*

Las Moras

Located a bit off the beaten path, but nevertheless an attractive restaurant featuring magnificent food. The specialty of the house is the chicken in garlic sauce. A comfortable terrace. *Open daily 1 pm–3 pm and 7 pm–2 am; C/. d'es Reguero, 4; Tel. 971 34 11 25; category 2*

Sa Prensa

A truly outstanding fish restaurant, where children are also very welcome. *Open daily noon–11 pm; C/. Marino Riquer, 9; Tel. 971 34 16 70; category 2*

Rías Baixas

★ Most certainly one of the best fish restaurants on the entire island. Galician cooking, known throughout Spain for its high standards, is here brought to perfection. The *Rías Baixas* is tucked away in an obscure side-street, not far from the old fortified church. Most of the diners are vacationing Spaniards and the local people. *Open daily 1.30 pm–4 pm and 8 pm–midnight; C/. Ignacio Riquer, 4; Tel. 971 34 04 80; category 1*

Hard-shelled delights out of the deep onto the table

Rincón de Pepe

This rather plain restaurant, which serves delicious *tapas* and splendid *mariscos*, provides a refreshing alternative to the usual run of tourist menus, grown predictable over time. *Open daily 1 pm–1 am; C/. Sant Mateu, 6; Tel. 971 34 06 9; category 3*

Es Siti

◉ A typical Spanish restaurant with international cuisine in the lively West End of Sant Antoni. The offerings are not especially varied, but inexpensive, and in any case better than what you get in the ordinary tourist restaurants in this part of town. *Open daily 1 pm–1 am; C/. Sant Antoni, 11a; Tel. 971 34 00 29; category 3*

SHOPPING

Es Bimbau

Specialises in Lladró porcelain. There is hardly anywhere else such a well-chosen array of goods. *C/. Ramón y Cajal, 8*

Sa Llara

Among the many things you can find in this tastefully-decorated shop are: handmade dolls, ceramic ware with Punic designs, wonderful prints for your wall in Ibizan designs, and presents guaranteed to please those you left behind. *C/. Sant Antoni, 20*

Markets

The market in Sant Antoni is housed in a modern building (there's even an escalator). It has more in common with one of those gigantic supermarkets than with a traditional Spanish marketplace. *C/. Progrés / C/. Mallorca*

May

The biggest department store in Sant Antoni. You'll find everything you need here. *C/. Sant Antoni, 13*

Panificadora Sant Antoni

Here is where you will find the famed *ensaimadas*, which, securely packed, often go back home with visitors as a sweet reminder of a holiday on Ibiza. *C/. Marino Riquer, 8 /C/. Progrés*

Newspapers

The best newspaper kiosk is where the road to Ibiza City crosses the road to Sant Josep. Foreign newspapers are often on sale here on the day they are published.

ACCOMMODATION

Nautilus

The only four-star hotel in Sant Antoni. Luxurious rooms, all of them with terrace and view of the cove. *C/. Port des Torrent/ Bahía de Sant Antoni; 168 rooms; Tel. 971 34 04 00, Fax 971 34 04 02; e-mail: h.montesol@ctv.es; category 1*

Pikes

★ This hotel, in a remote *finca*. has long been a secret of those in the know. Julio Iglesias sometimes rents the whole hotel to throw wild parties, which are fully reported in the next day's newspapers under large and lurid headlines. *Carretera Sa Vorera, km 12; 20 rooms; Tel. 971 34 22 22, Fax 971 34 23 12; e-mail: pikes@ctv.es; category 1*

Piscis Park

♁ Right on the esplanade that runs along the beach and in the immediate vicinity of a big disco. This hotel is for young people who want a lot of noise throughout the night. *C/. Miramar, no number; 366 rooms; Tel. 971 34 06 50, Fax 971 34 13 58; category 2*

Stella Maris

A charming holiday complex in a small sandy cove northwest of Sant Antoni. The apartments are large, and with balcony. *299 rooms; Cala Grassió; Tel. 971 34 06 00, Fax 971 34 27 31; e-mail: stmaris@ctv.es; category 2*

Vistabella

A bungalow complex with swimming pool and babysitting. All the bungalows are equipped with air-conditioning, satellite television, and telephone. *Camí de Benamussi, no number; Tel./Fax 971 34 33 97; e-mail: vistabella@ctv.es; category 2*

SPORTS & LEISURE

Perhaps because it is to be reached only at the end of a bumpy ride over a rough road, the ★ *Cala d'Hort* is seldom completely booked up, even in the middle of summer. The cove affords not only good bathing, but as well a good view of the two famed magic islands that lie off the Ibizan coast, Es Vedrá and Vedranell. If you are looking for a beach a bit more lively, you might drive to the *Cala Vedella* or even arrange to spend your whole holiday there right from the outset, in the club complex also called *Cala Vedella*. Other beaches farther to the north, the *Cala Molí*, the ★ *Cala Tarida*, and the *Cala Comte*, are all reachable by the excursion boat from Sant Antoni. Although these beaches attract rather a large crowd, they are among the cleanest on the island. The same cannot be said of the beaches in Sant Antoni Bay. The boat traffic there stirs up

The skyline of Sant Antoni de Portmany

the bottom too much, turning the water cloudy. To be recommended is the *Cala Salada*. This little bay is in a pleasant setting north of Sant Antoni and has a beach of fine sand and wonderfully clear water. It is easy to get there by bus or even on foot. And, unfortunately, by water as well. There is a brisk boat traffic from Sant Antoni to this place. Anyone looking for peace and quiet will be disappointed, because each excursion boat that lands here with its day-trippers stirs up a considerable amount of mud and sand.

There's a lot here for tennis players. Most of the big hotels have courts. Divers will find excellent instructors and good equipment in the *Sirena* diving centre. Its organises diving excursions to the island of Conejera. (*Diving Sport Centre Sirena, C/. Balanazat, 21 bajo; Tel. 971 34 29 66*).

ENTERTAINMENT

Suntanned gigolos, see-through blouses, very tiny bikinis, earbreaking music, and full cocktail glasses. When the sun sinks into the sea to the west, the excitement begins to rise in the West End of Sant Antoni. The night life here is not so extravagant and elegant as in Ibiza City, but no less effervescent and shrill. It's even louder here, and often more lively than in the bigger town.

They say that nowhere else are the nights longer and more torrid than here in Sant Antoni. When the beaches grow deserted towards evening, the West End, a small part of the Old Town, begins to fill up, mostly with young people. They come here because they cannot afford the admission fees charged by the discos in Ibiza City, which can come to as much as 30 U.S. dollars, or they simply don't want to pay such prices. And why should they? Not only is the night life definitely cheaper here in Sant Antoni, but as well the nights are especially noisy and turbulent, which is exactly what young people prefer.

One bar after the other tempts the punters with hamburgers, *copas*, and violently loud music.

Music bars, video bars, and disco bars — they say on Ibiza that the West End of Sant Antoni boasts the highest decibel level to be found on the island. Anyone who has ever experienced the pleasures of an evening in this place can tell you that that is no exaggeration. Take, for example, the Saturday nights during the summer months, when Spanish weekenders from the mainland mix with the local people. From 11 pm it begins to get fairly crowded in and in front of the bars. Intensive skin-contact is obligatory, as is the constant hammering of House and Techno and Heavy Metal. The clusters of people vibrate in time to the music, as do the flats over the bars where people live.

Sant Antoni has all the advantages and disadvantages of a youth scene. It is extremely loud, super-modern, and mad. This is a place for the weird, especially the young, to let off steam. And everyone knows in which bar he or she belongs. In the *Nightlife (C/. Santa Agnès, 1)* for example, the clientèle is almost exclusively British and twenty years young.

Two blocks further on you'll find that the patrons are overwhelmingly German-speaking. Two Berliners have set up a beer garden in the *Passeig Marítim* for those who would like to wash off the dust of a hot day with a couple of cold lagers. They call it *Pussycat – the Catastrophic Pub*. They have a great variety of beers here, which would be a catastrophe for the competition if there weren't a special clientèle exactly cut out for every bar. And the other way round.

In the *Café del Mar (C/. Lepanto)*, for example, you find more of what you might call a Smart Set: Trendy lads and classy girls in designer gear spend their hot nights here under their blow-dried coiffures. The music is some of the best and most up-to-date, and the view of the sea from the terrace is super.

Heavy Metal fans, on the other hand, tend to gather in the *Simple (C/. Santa Agnès, 2c)*. This video bar makes its impression purely by volume, an ear- and mind-numbing loudness to go with the many video screens hung around the place. Now and then rock greats on the order of Jimmy Page, of Led Zeppelin, will come through here.

One has a surfeit of choice when preparing to venture out into the night scene of Sant Antoni. From the disco bar *Sgt. Pepper (C/. de la Mar, 9d)* to the somewhat out-of-the-way *Casanova (C/. Sant Antoni, 17)*, to any one of the Techno spots — there's a gigantic array of dance joints where one can rave the long nights away. But one thing should be made clear: The action begins late. Before midnight, there's hardly a soul to be seen gyrating on any dance floor. Anyone who asks to be let in before 1 am is shown that he or she does not know how it works here, and can enjoy the dance floor all alone. It's generally around half past one when the first teenagers and twenty-somethings show up to enjoy the delights of the West End, for example in the ★ *Es Paradís,* the only serious competition the west coast has to offer the big discos of Ibiza City. But then they're off and running, in the Pyramid Disco in the *Travesía Dr. Fleming* and others. Flashing lights, lasers, and bodies all flicker among the palm trees till dawn. Locals mix with exotic foreigners on the dance floor, not least in the vain expectation of meeting a beautiful young prince with a bulging wallet.

Some people start their dancing as late as four in the morning in, for example, *Amnesia, a* disco that has been converted from a *finca* on the road from Sant Antoni to Ibiza City. A sort of soapy epiphany takes place here. At some point a vast mass of foam rolls out over the dance floor to the thudding beat of the bass speakers like something from a science fiction film. One can tell who has never been here before by the clueless look on their faces. But after a while everyone is thrashing about madly in the white bubble-bath. By sunrise only a small hard core of revellers remains. Some last it out because it's their first night, others because they are afraid that every night could be their last. Representatives of both groups meet on the beaches or in the super-modern disco *Space,* which opens its doors at seven in the morning. The tireless night people end their nightly round of pleasure in this disco only at noon. They have earned a rest until sunset...

INFORMATION

Oficina Municipal de Turismo
Open daily 9.30 am–1 pm and 4.30–7 pm; Tel. 971 34 33 63; Passeig de ses Fonts

SURROUNDING AREA

Capilla de Santa Agnès (101/D6)
This little underground chapel is about two km north of Sant Antoni. Legend has it that a nobleman donated a valuable picture of Saint Agnès to the village in gratitude for her intervention which saved his life during a terrible storm at sea. The bishop of the island granted him the right to built a chapel dedicated to Saint Agnès to hold the precious portrait. Although the chapel was never quite finished, the island people came here every year up to the 18th century to celebrate the name-day of Saint Agnès. In 1981, after the chapel had been neglected, almost forgotten, for more than 100 years, it was renovated with funds from the Ministry of Culture. The chapel has been accessible to visitors for some time now, if only twice a week. *(9 am–noon, Mon–Sat).*

To get there, follow the main road to Santa Agnès and turn right at the *Sa Capella de Can Basora.* You can walk to the chapel from the restaurant parking lot without any particular problems.

Formentera (108–109)
The boat trip from Sant Antoni to Formentera is without a doubt one of the most beautiful journeys possible on the many ferries that ply about the Pitiusas. The boat passes the islands of Conejera (where Hannibal is said to have been born) and Es Vedrá. *Leaves daily 10 am, return trip 2,800 pesetas)*

Santa Agnès (101/D–E4)
This little village to the north has for some time been con-

nected with Sant Antoni by regular rail service. A new bar has been opened for arriving rail visitors. If you have a few minutes after the trip, enjoy a glass of the local wine, not in the new *La Palmera*, but in the long-established *Bar Cosmi*. One can also drink in something of the traditional atmosphere of Ibiza here. As well as good wine, they have good mixed drinks. If you are still steady on your feet after all this, there is the possibility of a hike from Santa Agnès through fields and forest of the Ibizan north to the neighbouring village of Sant Mateu. You take the road behind the *Bar Cosmi* to the right, until you get to a fork in the road, when you take the right-hand way. Now you have a magnificent view of the valley spread out before you. After you have passed an olive plantation, you come across a small pine forest, and then the way is downhill towards Sant Mateu. This path is truly one of the most beautiful walks on the entire island.

Sant Mateu **(101/F4)**
This, the most unprepossessing village on the island, lies six km east of Santa Agnès, in the middle of a thoroughly rural district. Apart from the little church, the sports field, a little *tienda* and the obligatory bar, there is nothing to see here. Living proof that there are still villages on Ibiza that have not at all been disturbed by mass tourism.

SANT JOSEP

(104–105/C–D3) Sant Josep de sa Talaia, to give this place in south-western Ibiza its full name, is, if you go by area alone, the largest community on the island. It is worth a visit, simply because the approximately 10,000 inhabitants and their ways have not yet completely accommodated themselves to the tourist phenomenon. As for bars, you have a choice of two. The first is the *Bernat Vinya*, where the men, their berets pulled well down in back, meet on Sunday morning to play *manilla*, unlit cigarette stubs stuck in the corner of their mouths. The other is its modern counterpart, the *Cafetería Ruta*, with its snow-white tablecloths and brisk efficient service. After *café con leche*, take a stroll through the clean streets, and you will have a rough idea how life is lived these days in Ibizan villages. It is simple, direct, and traditional. Men and women, for example, seem to live separate existences, at least on the surface. You can see this in the church on Sundays, and afterwards, when the men repair to the café (no women there), and during the week, in the daily routine of work. The giant waves of tourism, which long since swamped most of the island, have not changed much of Sant Josep.

RESTAURANTS

Bar Bernat Vinya
This is a place for simple one-plate dishes and *raciones* (reduced portions). One of the smaller dishes is *tortilla española* (a potato omelette). With a little luck you might be invited to play cards with a group of Ibizans, an invitation that should not be turned

The traditional rural Ibiza survives in Sant Josep

down. The rules are quickly learned and the language problem seems to disappear after the third glass of red wine at the latest. *Daily 7 am–1 am; Pl. de sa Esglèsia, no number; Tel. 971 34 07 03; category 2*

Cana Joana
This is where Jean Michel Bamberger and his wife Joana serve good solid Catalan fare, which the Duke of Alba knew to appreciate. The restaurant is a little out of the way but worth the trip nevertheless. *Open daily 8 pm–midnight; Carretera Ciutat Eivissa–Sant Josep, km 10; Tel. 971 80 01 58; category 2*

SHOPPING

Artesanía Ca Vostra
One of the most beautiful shops of its sort on the Pitiusas. It features hand-made place mats, ceramics, porcelain vases, and the famed Spanish glassware. Here you can spend hours looking around. *Pedro Escanellas, no number*

Galería Sargantana
Gustavo Heberle shows and sells the impressive works of his wife Jussara, a well-known local painter. *Pl. de sa Esglèsia, no number*

ACCOMMODATION

Hacienda Cala Molí
A Swiss couple, the Freys, run this bungalow complex. One must book in writing. Right on the water. *Cala Molí; 8 rooms; Tel./Fax 971 80 60 02; category 2*

Ibiza Pueblo
A peaceful and clean hotel with swimming-pool bar, and television room. Children are welcome here. All rooms are equipped with air-conditioning. There is a small playground for the kids. *349 rooms; Port d'es Torrent; Tel. 971 34 05 12, Fax 971 34 00 55; e-mail: webmaster@barcelo.com; category 2*

Ayuntamiento

Information can be had from the mayor's office, since Sant Josep does not have its own tourist-information office. *Open 9 am– 2 pm Mon-Fri, 9 am–1.30 pm Sat; Tel. 971 34 33 63; C/. Pedro Escanellas, no number*

Cova Santa (105/D4)

Cova Santa is only a few metres away from the road to Ciutat Eivissa, about five km past Sant Josep. There are countless limestone caves all over the Pitiusas. Only a few of them, though, are open to visitors. One is at Cova Santa, and the Cova de Can Marça, in Port de Sant Miquel. *Open 9.30 am–1.30 pm and 3 pm– 7 pm Mon–Sat; admission 400 pesetas; Carretera Sant Josep–Ciutat Eivissa*

Sant Augustí (104–105/C-D2)

This village has grown into a proper German colony in the last few years. The *Bar Berri*, directly across from the church, is a meeting-place of German expatriates. The sole alternative for those who take no sauerkraut with their wine, but long for a Spanish dinner, is the restaurant called *Can Berri Vell (Tel. 971 34 43 21, category 2)*, which was established in 1986 in what is perhaps the oldest *finca* on Ibiza, on the Plaça de sa Església of Sant Augustí.

Sa Talaia (104/C3)

★ ⬇ The peak at Sa Talaia is 476 m high. If you decide to climb it, be sure to take along enough drinking water. But if you are not all that energetic, you can drive almost all the way to the top. Take the road going towards Sant Antoni and then follow the sign to Cala Vedella. After two km the road up to the peak turns off. Drive slowly along this very curvy road and keep an eye out for hazardous potholes as you go. Another dangerous thing is, after it rains, the road, often merely a track across fields, is sometimes barely negotiable. When that happens, there is always the footpath, slower but safer.

Es Vedrá (104/A-B4-5)

This enchanted island off the southwestern coast of Ibiza rises 382 m out of the sea. Es Vedrá and its little-sister island, Vedranell, form the centre of a skein of fantastic tales. To believe these stories, Es Vedrá, along with two places on Tortosa and Denia, is a sort of Bermuda Triangle. Carrier pigeons lose their sense of direction here, ships and airplanes mysteriously lose their way, and the stories of UFOs and their occupants fill archives. One of these tales is about an underwater station that the aliens are supposed to have built near Es Vedrá. Most holiday-makers, though, find the enchanting view from the Cala d'Hort, and the cool swim to be had there more interesting than the tales of missing ships and dizzy pigeons. In the event that you do want to visit Es Vedrá to find out what the stories are all about, simply take the Sunday ferry from Cala d'Hort. After you have satisfied your curiosity, you can eat in one of the truly excellent fish restaurants in the evening. (One is *Es Boldado; category 3*).

Just like the old days

The hours slip by more slowly between Sant Miquel and Cala Sant Vicent

The harsh wind blows over the road to Sant Miquel, and over the old Ibizan man in his dusty beret, a cigarette end in his mouth, on the way home on his spindle-legged old donkey. A fairly unusual picture for most parts of Ibiza these days. But in the northern part of the island, between Cala Sant Vicent and Sant Miquel, life goes by almost as it did in grandmother's time. There are, it's true, some giant concrete tourist complexes near the beach here, but luckily only in a few places. Port de Sant Miquel, Portinatx, and Cala Sant Vicent are the only tourist centres in this otherwise thinly populated part of Ibiza, with its craggy forbidding coastline, which affords only limited bathing facilities. The sheltered bathing cove of Port de Sant Miquel, little Cala Xarraca, and the three sandy beaches of Portinatx, so close together that they almost run into

The northern part of Ibiza, little frequented by tourists, exercises its magic spell over mystics and those fascinated by the esoteric

each other. The Cala de Sant Vicent all have, granted, a spectacular setting, but they cannot be compared with the broad beaches and deserted dunes that one finds at Ses Salines.

The north is best avoided by anyone who comes to Ibiza to party through the night. A deathly silence hangs over this region after midnight. On the other hand, it is an ideal place to relax completely. Three places, Sant Miquel, Sant Llorenç, and Sant Joan, all of them somewhat removed from the life of the coast and the beaches, are worth visiting if you want to get an utterly different impression of the island. In Sant Miquel, for instance, the local folklore groups have for years afforded visitors an insight into traditional Ibizan dance and music. Another, completely different sort of movement has more recently surfaced, in Sant Joan. In the 1960s, the hippies came to Ibiza to preach and live out their idealistic notions of a better, more honest world, of a life worth living. Now we see another type of person on the island, interested principally in self-knowledge and the esoteric. Some of these newer arrivals are former adherents of the Bhagwan guru who left the USA in the wake of that movement's ignoninious collapse.

SANT JOAN

(102/C3) Sant Joan de Labritja, to give it its full name, with barely 4,000 inhabitants, lies the centre of the north, and is the hub of the world for the people of this region. The few tourists who wander into the north at first take Sant Joan for a sleepy little nest. The proud Catalan flag hangs limply from its staff in front of the town hall, and the half-dozen sentries on duty at the Guardia Civil barracks seem more interested in the chances of a siesta than in anything else. This first impression, of a God-forsaken hole at the end of nowhere, of a dreariness and tedium beyond telling, is the impression taken away by those who stop here for a fast cup of coffee on their way to the beaches of the north coast.

But if one takes a little time to look around, one will learn that things do go on here. Unusual for Ibiza, it was not mass tourism that got things moving in Sant Joan. Whatever bars, restaurants, and shops there are, are here because of the needs of the local people. There are two establishments that will serve as good examples of the way things have changed. One is the *Eivissa Communication Organization (ECO),* that offers assistance and support of various sorts to residents and those who desire to become residents. The other is the *New Age Bazar,* a few doors further on in the same street. They are described under SHOPPING in this chapter. Enjoyment of life expresses itself in a different way in Sant Joan than in Ibiza City or Sant Antoni. This is one reason why those tourists who must have constant variety and change will do well to give the place a wide berth. Others, though, will feel quite at home amidst the even and peaceful flow of life as it is lived in Sant Joan. These peo-

MARCO POLO SELECTION: THE NORTH COAST

1 Can Gall
A restaurant located in an old *finca* (page 65)

2 Sant Miquel
Weekly folklore performances on the square in front of the church (page 69)

3 Cova de Can Marça
The old smugglers' cave in the bay of Port de Sant Miquel (page 69)

4 Cala Xarraca
This is where they shot the outdoor scenes of the Hollywood musical 'South Pacific' (page 66)

5 New Age Bazar
Signs of times to come? (page 65)

6 Hacienda Na Xamena
The most luxurious hotel on the Pitiusas (page 66)

ple should plan to stay longer than it takes to gulp down a hasty *café con leche*. Those who like the town can appreciate the fact that even the somewhat disreputable-looking Guardia Civiles here are friendly and not at all the type to pull out a book of tickets every time they see a car illegally parked.

RESTAURANTS

Balafia
A lovely outdoor restaurant. Specialties are grilled fowl and delicious rabbit. Large portions. *Carretera Sant Joan, km 15.4; no Tel.; category 3*

Can Gall
★ Diners on the terrace have, in the evening, a splendid view of the illuminated church of Santa Eulària on the hilltop. Two things that keep the regulars coming back to *Can Gall* are the first-class cuisine and an excellent wine list. *Open 1–3.30 pm and 8–11 pm Wed–Mon; Carretera Portinatx, km 11.6; Tel. 971 33 29 16; category 2*

Vista Alegre
The name means something like 'The Merry Glance'. Over the years this sleepy little place with its overgrown terrace has turned into an efficient restaurant with an enclosed winter garden. *Open daily 10 am–midnight; Pl. d'Espanya, no number, no Tel.; category 3*

SHOPPING

Cachiaches
Features second-hand goods, all the way from old washstands to leather jackets. *Pl. d'Espanya, no number*

ECO
The *Eivissa Communication Organization* performs a number of services. The people there will run your household for you, take telephone calls and pass them on, perform computer transactions, and arrange for flights back home. The north's best source of information of all kinds. You can even hire a car from the *ECO. Pl. d'Espanya, no number*

New Age Bazar
★ Books on the esoteric, relaxation courses, astrology courses, instruction in the tarot. In short, something for everyone interested in the New Self-Realisation. *Pl. d'Espanya, no number*

ACCOMMODATION

Cala Sant Vicent   (103/E3)
A mid-range hotel especially popular with families travelling with children. There is a lot for small children in particular here. Right on the beach. *Cala Sant Vicent; 120 rooms; Tel. 971 33 00 21, Fax 971 33 00 60; category 2*

Cas Mallorquí   (102/C2)
This unpretentious but well-run hotel is directly on the beach at Portinatx. People travelling on their own, without a group, find it ideal. *Cala de Portinatx, 28; 11 rooms; Tel. 971 33 30 67; category 3*

Cigüeña Playa   (102/C2)
A hotel in the lower price category, situated about 30 metres from the beach on a slight rise. Swimming pool and terrace. *Cala de Portinatx; 84 rooms; Tel. 971 32 62 14, Fax 971 32 06 16; category 3*

Galeón/Cartago (102/B3)

Two spectacular hotels that seem to have grown directly out of the rocky shoreline. *Port de Sant Miquel; 182/196 rooms; Tel. 971 33 45 51, Fax 971 33 45 32; category 2*

Hacienda Na Xamena (102/B3)

★ The only five-star hotel on the Pitiusas. It towers almost 200 m over the bay of Port de Sant Miquel. All the things you've ever imagined in a dream hotel are to be had here. Little boutiques, first-class restaurants, and several swimming pools that make up for the lack of a beach. *Urbanización Na Xamena, Port de Sant Miquel; 59 rooms; Tel. 971 33 45 00, Fax 971 33 45 14; e-mail: hl.hacienda@vlc.servicom.es; category 1*

Imperio Playa (103/E3)

A three-star hotel next to a small shopping centre. The hotel has its own disco. *Cala Sant Vicent; 210 rooms; Tel. 971 33 30 55; category 2*

Presidente Playa (102/C2)

A superior mid-range hotel with swimming pool, minigolf, and children's playground. The hotel has its own hairdresser's. *Cala de Portinatx; 270 rooms; Tel. 971 32 05 76, Fax 971 32 32 57; category 1*

Se Vinye (102/C2)

One shouldn't expect too much of the *Se Vinye*, but on the other hand the prices are reasonable. *Cala de Portinatx; 11 rooms; Tel. 971 32 05 40; category 3*

SPORTS & LEISURE

The smaller beaches of the north do not have a lot to offer by way of water sports. There is the ★ *Cala Xarraca*, quite near Portinatx and a bit apart from the highly developed tourist beaches. The countryside here was at one point especially favoured by Hollywood film-makers. And it was here, close to the bay, that they filmed the outside shots of the musical 'South Pacific'.

There are three beaches in Portinatx itself that are more or less cut off from each other by cliff formations that jut out into the water. They are *S'Arenal Petit*, *S'Arenal Gran*, and *Es Port*.

S'Arenal Petit und S'Arenal Gran together are too small to accommodate the hordes of tourists that descend in summer. The holiday visitors are positively stacked along the beach in July and August, and the water gets dirty and cloudy. But the water-ski centre at the northern end of S'Arenal Gran offers an alternative to simply lying around. If you are at all interested in the underwater world, but don't want to bother with diving gear, a trip on the glass-bottomed boat is the answer.

Es Port is the northernmost bathing cove of Portinatx. Its natural harbour lies in a protected location and so is a good place to take children. There is a diving centre here where the well-trained staff will help beginners and experienced divers get to know the colourful underwater world of the rugged northern coast. This diving centre is one of the best on the island. Everything is done here in a professional manner.

ENTERTAINMENT

There is practically no night life in the north, apart from the discos in the hotels. It must be said, however, that the hotels go to great effort for their guests, and, like the big discos in Ibiza City and Sant Antoni, organise various competitions and special fiestas. Yet it must be said that most of these occasions are rather forced. It is better to go to Ibiza City for real entertainment, and spend some time in *Es Paradís, Pacha* or in one of the other discotheques. But you'll need some form of transport. Do take care on the return trip from a night's disco-dancing. There are so many blind curves on this extremely tricky road that great attention and alertness are called for. The sight of the many old and new wrecks in the ditch alongside the road should be warning enough.

INFORMATION

Sant Joan doesn't have its own information bureau, but with a little Spanish you can find out what you need at the mayor's office. You may even have a chat with the mayor himself. He holds office hours three times a week, when he chats with everyone and anyone turns up. Holiday guests are welcome; you will be received informally and without bureaucratic obstacles. *Ayuntamiento (mayor's office); noon–2 pm Mon, Wed, Fri; town hall offices open for business noon–1.30 pm Mon-Sat; Pl. de sa Esglèsia, no number; Tel. 971 33 30 03*

SURROUNDING AREA

Cala Sant Vicent   (103/D–E3)

The bus runs only twice a day between Cala Sant Vicent and the cove of the same name to Ibiza City. While there is not much to Cala Sant Vicent itself, there are some quiet hotels along the bay, and a fair few pleasant restaurants and cafes. The approach to ✶ Cala de Sant Vicent is full of curves, so exercise great care at the wheel. Your reward will be a truly breathtaking view of the bay and the cliffs of

Hotel complexes at Cala Sant Vicent, not really typical of the north

A bathing cove in Portinatx, the north's stronghold of tourism

the coastline. The clean and well-tended beach is about 400 m long, and in spite of all the hotels, apartment complexes, bars, and restaurants in the area the water is clean. The way to the nearby *Cova d'es Cuilleram* has been partly signposted for the convenience of visitors. But the cave itself is not yet accessible, nor is there any fixed date for its opening.

Portinatx   (102–103/C–D2)

Don't worry about the pronunciation of the name of this place. Just say 'Portinatch'. That's how the locals say it. This place with the funny name is the northernmost holiday resort on Ibiza. The coast is lined with cliffs hereabouts, and the different bathing beaches are cut off from one another by points of land formed by the cliffs. There are in all four beaches: *Sa Torre, S'Arenal Petit, S'Arenal Gran,* and *Es Port.* They are all fairly close to one another and easy to reach by foot. If one or the other is full up,

which happens frequently in summer, one can easily walk to the next. Portinatx itself seems to have sprung directly out of the ground, one hotel after another set down without remorse. Once-deserted bays with crystal-clear water have turned into overcrowded sunbathing terraces with cloudy water, all of this of course in the name of tourism development. There are of course no older buildings to be seen here. No fortified church, not one typical Ibizan country pub, things which even the most remote village can proudly point to. Before they built the hotels, there was nothing here except cliffs, a few deserted sandy coves *(calas)*, and the sea. The coast is rather forbidding here. The cliffs make an excursion to the beach in many places a mountain-climbing expedition, so people tend to stick to the developed beaches and do not explore the area looking for new places to swim. The better you are at hiking, the better your chances of finding a small, remote place to spread your towel.

Portinatx is so out of the way that even day-trips to Ibiza City and other parts of the island become involved affairs. There is regular bus service, but the buses are so few and far between that one is better off hiring a car or a motor scooter to get away from Portinatx for a few hours. But at any rate, the only reason for coming to the north in the first place is to find peace and quiet, They have both here, in great measure.

Sant Llorenç   (102/B–C4)

This tiny village is nothing more than a handful of houses clustered around the parish church. The historical site *Balàfia* is quite close. The Moorish towers at Balàfia bear witness to the centuries-long rule of the Arabs on the island. One km east of Sant Llorenç, on the route to Sant Joan, is the ✪ restaurant *Es Pins*, very popular among the local people. *Carretera Sant Joan, km 14.8; Tel. 971 33 32 16; open daily except Wed 7 am–midnight; category 3*

Sant Miquel   (102/B3–4)

★ This place is best known for its traditional folklore and imposing fortified church (16th century). Local folklore groups perform traditional music and dances during the summer months on the square in front of the church, in the open air. The performances take place every Thursday at 6 pm. Tourists flock to Sant Miquel from all parts of the island to see these shows. There are even special buses laid on from Ibiza City. These

performances last for about one hour. The music and dances (in folk costume) are usually the same ones that are performed during village festivals. The Curta, the Larga, the Nueve Vueltas, the Cambio de Parejas and others are danced to the sound of instruments handed down from generation to generation. The principal ones are flute, castanets, drums, the *espasi* (triangle) and the *xeremía,* a sort of flute that came to the Pitiusas from ancient Egypt. At the end, the performance turns into a small Ibizan festival accompanied by *vino pagés.* Apart from these Thursdays, Sant Miquel is quite peaceful, since tourists hardly ever stop here in the normal course of events. They usually drive straight to the coast, to the beach at Port de Sant Miquel, where there are several attractive holiday complexes and hotels built into the cliffs. Worthy of note here is the ⬥ ★ *Cova de Can Marça,* a cave about 100,000 years old, later used by smugglers and now open to visitors. *(Tours every hour; admission 800 pesetas).* Quite near Port de Sant Miquel is the most exclusive hotel on the island, the *Hacienda Na Xamena,* perched on 200-m cliffs overlooking the sea. A sometimes risky path leads down to the *Platja de Na Xamena,* a beach cut deep into the cliff face where the water is crystal clear. The beach is not large, but is never crowded, because it is so hard to get to. The *Hacienda Na Xamena* and the surrounding bays are often used as the spectacular background for films, Spanish- and foreign-made.

The land of your dreams

Here's the spot for alternative lifestyles as well as tourist accommodations sensibly set in the landscape

The road to the shore and its beach umbrellas weaves through green pine forest and ochre fields. The sea is deep blue and provides a contrast to the dazzling white of the bungalows along the coast. Even if Ibiza's east coast is a little too built-over with apartment blocks, one has the feeling that it has all been carried out with some forethought and taste. The guests of the club complexes hidden amid pine groves are put up in little bungalows rather than in gigantic concrete termitehills. At the same time, there are lots of things to do that provide for many vacationers a welcome break from suntanning and swimming. The largest place in the eastern part of Ibiza is Santa Eulària, a model of how a locality should grow to meet the needs of tourism without at the same time completely sacrificing its original identity. In Santa Eulària they have learnt that tourists are not satisfied with the simpler pleasures alone. Accordingly, there is in the immediate vicinity, in Roca Llisa, the only (to date, at least) golf course on the island, which was enlarged to 18 holes at the beginning of the 1990s. They have also planned the first big harbour for pleasure boats outside Ibiza City, in the northeastern part of Santa Eulària Bay. But there is quite another reason why people flock to the east. The oldest, largest, and best-known hippie market on the island takes place there every Wednesday, on the grounds of the Punta Arabí holiday complex in Es Caná. And whoever is interested in the history of the 1960s and 1970s on Ibiza should pay a visit to the tiny community of Sant Carles, six km north of Santa Eulària. The village is still a meeting-place for the greying hippies who come to the northeastern part of Ibiza to dream on about another, better world.

The mediaeval fortified church atop the 66-metre high Puig de Missa, visible for miles around, is the symbol of Eulària d'es Riu

SANTA EULÀRIA

(**107/D1**) Santa Eulària d'es Riu, with 14,000 inhabitants, is the

MARCO POLO SELECTION: THE EAST COAST

1 Anita's Bar
Bar, communications centre, and meeting-place of the last hippies (page 79)

2 The hippie market in Punta Arabí
The biggest and oldest hippie market on the island (page 75)

3 Las Dalias
Marketplace, café and rock theatre (page 79)

4 Passeig Marítim
The esplanade along the shore at Santa Eulària (page 73)

5 Puig de Missa
The largest fortified church on the Pitiusas (page 73)

6 Roca Llisa
The only 18-hole golf course on the Pitiusas, and very exclusive (page 77)

largest town in the east. The town's subtitle, as one might call it, d'es Riu, derives from the river that, in principle at least, empties into the sea here. But you will search for the river itself in vain. Most of the rivers in the Pitiusas have dried up to a great extent because the water table has sunk considerably. This development, caused by the increasing numbers of tourists on the islands, continues, and gets worse each year as more and more tourists arrive. Today, all there is to see is the dried-up riverbed. You cross over it a little before you arrive in Santa Eulària on the way from Ibiza City. It is from this bridge that you have the best view of the symbol of Santa Eulària, the fortified church standing high over the town on the ꝏ Puig de Missa. The church was built in 1235, after the Reconquista, on the ruins of a mosque. The walk up the hill is indeed tiring, nevertheless, it's worth the effort. From the top you have an exten-

sive view of Santa Eulària and the surrounding communities. But don't forget to take a look at the churchyard. Here, as everywhere in Spain, the dead are not buried, but placed in tombs above ground. Some of these tombs are five storeys high. When you read the names on the tombs, you can see that many foreign residents have found their final resting-places here.

The Germans have been the largest group of visitors to Santa Eulària d'es Riu for years now. They like, among other things, the mixture of the traditional and the touristic to be found here. Santa Eulària is a peaceful sort of place. There are some cocktail bars and even a disco, but those interested in night life get only a dampened version of it here. On the contrary, visitors to this place know the value of orderly, quiet surroundings. The creature comforts top the list here. It is not difficult to find something of a Central European atmosphere in this small place, even in the details of daily life. Part of this feeling is in the ritual afternoon coffee and tea (complete with cakes) and a draught beer in the evening. An extraordinarily attractive prospect is the esplanade along the beach, which extends from the Ramblas to the new yacht harbour. Bars and restaurants invite one to tarry along the esplanade, called the ★ *Passeig Marítim*.

SIGHTS

Ramblas

❂ The Ramblas is the place for a leisurely stroll in Santa Eulàrias, as elsewhere in Spain. Friends meet for a chat here during the regular Sunday-afternoon promenade; and this is where one can buy a newspaper to read in peace in the shade of the old trees that line the way. The Ramblas connects the main thoroughfare of Santa Eulària, the *Carrer Sant Jaume,* with the new esplanade, mentioned above. If you

turn right into the esplanade at the end of the Ramblas, you enter the newer part of town, with its modern shops and blocks of flats. If you turn left, you will soon pass a whole series of new cocktail bars, and the restaurant *Doña Margarita*. A few hundred metres farther along, you will see the new yacht harbour.

Fortified Church and Museum

★ ◁▷ The 66-metre-high symbol of Santa Eulària, its fortified church, surveys the town from the Puig de Missa. The walls of this whitewashed and gleaming 14th-century church are several metres thick. It was often used as a place of refuge by the people of the town during attacks by pirates and other seagoing marauders. The cannons that once graced the roof of the church are no longer there. This is the most beautiful and best-preserved example of the fortified churches so typical of the Pitiusas. It is often closed during the week. If

There's room to stroll in the shade of the old trees along the Ramblas of Santa Eulària

you want to take a look inside, wait until Sunday, or just before or after early Mass on weekdays. The cemetery of Santa Eulària, just next the church, has the usual Spanish above-ground tombs. Ibiza's only ethnological museum is just behind the churchyard, in a restored farmhouse. *Open daily 11 am–1 pm and 5–8 pm; admission free*

RESTAURANTS

Andaluza

Fish, *tapas* and delicious ham are served up in this tavern, painted a bright festive blue. Highly recommended. *Open 12.30 pm– midnight; C/. Sant Vicent, 51; Tel. 971 33 91 56; category 3*

El Bigote

There's no telephone here, so you have to go in person before noon to order your lunch. Freshly caught fish is the main specialty in this small family-run enterprise. The food is good and the prices reasonable. *Open daily from noon to 3 pm; Cala Mastella, Sant Carles; category 3*

Es Caliú

Steak and lamb grilled over an open wood fire are the specialties offered by Vicente Escardell. The restaurant is a few km outside Santa Eulària, to the west, so you'll need a car to get there. *Open daily except Mon 1–3.30 pm and 8–11 pm; Carretera Ciutat Eivissa–Sant Joan, km 11; Tel. 971 33 13 68; category 2*

Can Miquel

An excellent fish restaurant with an extensive selection. *Open daily 12.30–3 pm and 8–11.30 pm;* C/. Sant Vicent, 43; Tel. 971 33 03 29; category 2*

Can Pepe Salvado

The local inhabitants in particular are fond of this restaurant, located a little outside Santa Eulària. There's a crowd there before the summer season and after it's over too. *Open daily 1– 3 pm and 7–11 pm; Carretera Es Canà, km 1.2; category 2*

Celler Can Pere

Old wine barrels and a big fireplace help create the traditional atmosphere of this restaurant. The owner, Paco, knows exactly what to do with freshly caught fish, shellfish, and *jabugo*, a variety of ham. *Open daily 1 pm– midnight; C/. Sant Jaume; Tel. 971 33 00 56; category 2*

Doña Margarita

A comfortable place with Catalan and international cuisine on the gourmet level. *Open daily 7 pm– midnight; Passeig Marítim, no number; Tel. 971 33 22 00; category 1*

Es Farallo

Rabbit is the specialty of this open-air restaurant. *Open daily 7 pm–midnight; Carretera Es Canà, km 0.7; Tel. 971 33 07 85; category 2*

La Noria

The diners feast on fresh fish and seafood on a terrace overlooking the sea. Especially reasonable as well. *Open daily noon–4 pm; Cala Boix, Sant Carles; no Tel.; category 3*

La Posada

The *Posada* is on the way to Puig de Missa. The owner, from mainland Spain, has remodeled an old *finca* and made an attractive restaurant out of it. During the winter months one dines not on the terrace but in the large inner room, as near as possible to the fireplace, which gives off a cheery glow. *Open daily except Tue 7 pm–1 am; C'an Fluxa d'es Puig de Missa, no number; Tel. 971 33 00 17; category 2*

La Rambla

As the name would suggest, the restaurant is to be found on the Ramblas of Santa Eulària. The Spanish owners learned their trade in Switzerland. It's best to go all the way through the restaurant to the marvelous garden at the rear. *Open daily except Mon noon–3 pm and 6.30 pm–11.30 pm; Passeig S'Alamera, 18; Tel. 971 33 08 57; category 2*

SHOPPING

Centre d'Art – Artesanía de Ibiza

This is the place where you can find handmade *objets d'art 34* at all price levels. *C/. Isidor Macabich, 34*

Cerámica típica

This little shop is situated in a normal block of flats with green shutters on the windows. It doesn't look in any way special from the street, and if you're not careful you'll walk right by it. Once you get inside, you will find ceramic ware for everyday use at acceptable prices. *C/. Sant Josep, 25*

The Hippie Market

★ Ibiza's best-known and largest hippie market is held on Wednesdays on the grounds of the *Punta Arabí* club. It goes on all day. *Es Caná*

Mari Juan Meubles

It's marvelous fun to look around in this one-of-a-kind furniture shop. Even if you can't buy anything, or don't want to, it is worth poking your nose in for a peek. The many different sorts of things here are oddly attractive. *C/. Sant Josep, 51*

The Market

The general market, as lively as it is popular, is behind the *Carrer Sant Josep*, on the way to Puig de Missa. You can get pretty well everything to eat here, from fresh fruit and vegetables to meat and freshly caught fish. *C/. del Sol*

Salewski's Butcher Shop

The sausage here is guaranteed to be without garlic. All the sliced sausage is made according to German recipes by Werner Salewski and provides for many of the resident foreigners here a welcome change from the Spanish *chorizo*, which is usually air-dried and hard as a rock. *Passeig S'Alamera, no number*

Newspapers and Books

You won't find any really good bookshops *(librerías)* in Santa Eulària. But you will find a great many large newspaper kiosks that not only carry the international papers, most of them on the day of publication, but as well a limited selection of light novels in English. The most important of these kiosks, for tourists, is on the *Passeig S'Alamera,* the Ramblas. One of the larger bookshops is the *Librería Cosmi, C/. Sant Jaume, 62*

Es Alocs

North of Santa Eulària is the vast and utterly clean beach called the Platja d'es Figueral. The *Hostal Es Alocs*, a reasonably-priced family-run pension, offers simple but adequate accommodation. *Platja d'es Figueral; Tel. 971 33 50 79; category 3*

S'Argamassa

A large hotel in the upper price-range, four km from the centre of Santa Eulària. Swimming pool and other water sports. *Urbanización S'Argamassa; 217 rooms; Tel./Fax 971 33 00 76; category 1*

Cala Llonga

The flat bottom here makes this beach a good one for children. One can walk out into the water for quite some distance before it gets at all deep. The *Cala Llonga* has all the usual things that a vacationer cannot bear to think of doing without. *Cala Llonga; 163 rooms; Tel. 971 19 65 01, Fax 971 19 65 13; e-mail: director@ibiza-hotels. com; category 2*

Can Curreu

A hotel set in an old farmhouse near Sant Carles. Well-decorated, comfortable rooms, all with whirl-pool baths, television, air-conditioning, and fireplace. As well, the hotel has a swimming pool, a sauna, and a solarium. *Carretera Sant Carles, km 12; Tel./Fax 971 33 52 80; e-mail: Can-Curreu@ibiza-online.com; category 1*

Ses Estaques

A mid-range hotel year the yacht harbour. It has a mini-golf course, tennis courts, and a swimming pool. *Ses Estaques;*

Right on the beach: the holiday village Punta Arabí

159 rooms; Tel. 971 33 02 00, Fax 971 33 04 86; category 2

Punta Arabí Holiday Club

⚑ Young people in particular enjoy this club complex, which is equipped with an extensive array of leisure and exercise facilities. On Wednesday the hippie market, known all over Ibiza, is held on the grounds. *Punta Arabí, Es Caná; Tel. 971 33 06 50, Fax 971 33 91 67; e-mail: parabi@jet.es; category 3*

Hacienda Encanto del Río

A comfortable little hotel with individually decorated apartments, very comfortable. *Apartado 197, Sant Carles; Tel. 971 32 00 06; e-mail: encanto@ibiza-online.com; category 1*

Pereyra Internacional

Small but good, this luxurious inn with the usual amenities. All rooms come with waterbed, satellite television, and minibar. *Carretera Santa Eulària, km 2; Tel./Fax 971 33 26 43; category 1*

Les Terrasses

This remodeled *finca* has only six double rooms, but every one has been personally decorated by the owner, Françoise Pialoux. *Carretera Santa Eulària, km 1, La Piedra Azul; Tel./Fax 971 33 26 43; category 1*

SPORTS & LEISURE

The best opportunities for water sports are along the beaches north of Santa Eulària, on Punta Arabí and in the *Cala Pada*. There are surfing lessons for beginners. Those who already know how to handle themselves in the surf can hire the boards on their own. There is good swimming on the broad but fairly crowded sandy beach called *Platja d'es Figueral* in the well-tended *Cala Llenya*, and the very lively *Cala Pada* (in the general area of Punta Arabí/Es Caná). The *Cala Llonga,* south of Santa Eulària, is also good, especially for children, because it has a shallow bottom. There is a club for those not particularly fond of the water, the *Punta Arabí;* it runs stables that organise equestrian outings in the surrounding countryside. An hour's riding instruction costs around 2,000 pesetas. The only golf course on the island (so far) is in ★ *Roca Llisa*, south of Santa Eulària *(Club de Golf; Tel. 971 31 37 18)*. Guests are welcome, but must belong to a recognised golf club. Caddies are available, and there are clubs for hire. You can play all day for 4,000 pesetas.

ENTERTAINMENT

Night life here is limited to a few bars, none of them really remarkable. If you are after good entertainment, it is better to leave Santa Eulària after dinner for another destination. It appears that the bars, and the shops as well, are not doing as well as they could, as little by little life is steadily becoming more lively elsewhere. But for those who want to get to know Santa Eulària by night, here are the most important addresses.

Athenea

Ice cream, cake, cocktails and apéritifs are the specialties of this establishment, located directly on the beach. *Passeig Marítim*

Crocodil Bar

Lots of atmosphere, lots of music and lots of young people. They meet here to chat and have a drink. Many of the regulars come here not least for the delicious cocktails, served by pretty waitresses. *Open 8 pm–4 am Wed–Mon; C/. de sa Església*

Discos

There is a whole series of smaller discos outside Santa Eulària, none of which can compare with *Privilege* or *Pacha* in Ibiza City. Two of these smaller places are *Estudio 64* in Sant Llorenç, and *Hollywood*, in Cala Llonga. But it is possible after all to have fun in these places, even if they are not as spectacular as the bigger discos.

Doña Ana

Delicious *tapas, copas* and a hearty atmosphere characterise this bar at the pleasure-boat harbour. One can play billiards and pinball, drink and chat here well into the early-morning hours. And all this with a tremendous view of the sea. What more could one desire? *Puerto Deportivo*

Fred's Bar

You wouldn't find a more typical English pub in London itself. No wonder most of the regulars here are British. It's often very convivial, and there's often a lot of loud singing. There's no lack of merriment, and no lack of draught Guinness either. *Pl. d'Espanya, no number*

Royalty

A biggish place, a bar and coffee house that take up almost an entire building. In the last few years it has not only been considerably enlarged but has also taken on a much more international flavour, at the expense of the Spanish atmosphere, that is. In spite of all this, though, the bar is still one of the 'classics' of Santa Eulària. *Pl. d'Espanya, no number*

Sinatra's Cafeteria

Don't be fooled by the cafeteria part of the name. You can get more than coffee here; there's a full breakfast menu and other things, up to and including cream cakes. But the best time in *Sinatra's* is at night, when you sit and sip a Coco Loco or a Piña Colada, the mainstays of the cocktail list. In the evenings lots of young people meet here to talk and laugh and enjoy life in general. *Passeig Marítim*

INFORMATION

Oficina de Información y Turismo
9.30 am–1.30 pm Mon–Sat and 4:30–7 pm on Fri; Tel. 971 33 07 28; C/. Ignasi Wallis, 4

SURROUNDING AREA

Es Caná   (103/E5)

This place has become generally known because of the hippie market held on Wednesday on the grounds of the *Punta Arabí* club. The attractions of the club itself are tailored almost exclusively to the needs and desires of young people. There are exercise programmes, surfing classes and picnic excursions by boat known as pirate voyages. The up-to-date camping ground has all imaginable conveniences. There are some restaurants in Es Caná itself. Of these, *La Jacaranda* is especially worth mentioning. *(Tel. 971 33 93 48; category 3).* The whitewashed restaurant owes some of its atmosphere to its situation on a little prominence overlooking the sea. Set a little apart from the beach is the *Zodiak,* whose main attraction is its pool. One can have a refreshing swim before dinner. *(admission 325 pesetas).* If you like Chinese food, try the *Mandarin,* entirely painted in Chinese red. The atmosphere is typically Chinese, the service friendly and helpful, and the food good.

Sant Carles de Peralta (103/D-E4)

What Sant Ferràn de ses Roques is to Formentera, Sant Carles is to Ibiza. Like Sant Ferràn, Sant Carles has its bar 'where everything began', ★ *Anita's Bar.* Anita's to this day serves as a communications centre, postal-box address, pub, and meeting-place for the ex-hippies and Beautiful People who are living in remote *fincas* in the northeast. Erwin Bechthold was a regular at Anita's

in the 1960s. The children of the Woodstock generation have made some adjustments in their high ideals over the years. Many of them are now crafty businesspeople. They organise some sensational events, sometimes in *Anita's,* but more often in ★ *Las Dalias,* a few km away. These fairs are a mixture of bar, café, art show, marketplace and concert hall. The beaches around Sant Carles are hard to reach, and backed by cliffs. That is the situation at *Aigua Blanca* Bay, one of the two official nudist beaches on the island.

La Siesta (106–107/C–D1)

This apartment complex is a particular favourite of German holiday-makers. There is a very good selection of bars and cafes. A tip: *La Paella (Tel. 971 33 09 02; category 2)* has good food and a pleasant atmosphere. The terrace is covered with flowering vines. Next to the restaurant is a place that offers a lot of opportunities for sport, including a riding stables. The holiday village's beach, *Caló de S'Alga,* is fairly small and rocky.

The harbour at Es Caná welcomes visitors by sea and by land

A placid Mediterranean paradise

Formentera will put you under its spell right from the first starlit evening walk

The windmill at El Pilar creaks as it turns slowly in the wind, and a farmer ploughs his dusty fields with a antiquated tractor and the patience of a saint. Life proceeds at a more leisurely pace on Formentera than on Ibiza. This is an island for individualists and for all those who, while on holiday at least, do not require everything to happen at once. Difficulties and grumbling on a trip to Formentera can arise as early as the sea voyage from Ibiza. You have in front of you a ferry trip of one hour (25 minutes by jetfoil) to La Savina, the port of Formentera. The trip is not long enough for your stomach to get accustomed to the sea, and not short enough to avoid stomach problems entirely. Even in good weather, the wind and waves can be enough to rock the

Two hundred metres above the sea, the lighthouse on Punta de sa Ruda dominates the craggy coastline at La Mola

ferry so that the trip is uncomfortable, to say the least. But once you get to Formentera, you will be rewarded for your toil and trouble. The peace and quiet here, unless you have just come from the Highlands of Scotland or deepest Montana, will positively astound you. You will be surprised at how little noise there can be, even during the day, because so many people here travel by bicycle. Another key experience is your first night on Formentera. Be sure to go out for a walk after the sun sets, to let the night sky, with its clear starlight, not dispersed by street lamps, work its magic. Soon the enchantment of Formentera will have worked its spell on you. You will come to feel sorry for the day-trippers who take a short excursion from Ibiza to the little-sister island. They have to go back at 6 pm, when the last ferry leaves. Life moves along in a decidedly pleasant way on Formentera. But at the same time, it is never boring here. The island is large enough to offer something to do every day. Wonderful beaches with turquoise water, such as the Platja Ses Illetas or the ★ *Platja de Mitjorn* (**108-109/C-D5**); small but lively communities with their own character, such as Sant Ferràn and Sant Francesc; El Pilar and La Mola at the extreme eastern end of the island; a prehistoric gravesite, a Roman settlement, and deep caves to explore, complete with stalactites and stalagmites. All this is more than one could do in any two-week vacation. The best part is that you can easily undertake all these excursions by bicycle. There are bike-rental places everywhere, and their prices are reasonable. Have you got small children with you? No problem, these rental shops will bolt on a child's seat in a twinkling. The topography of the is-land is so obvious that you will seldom need a map. Strictly speaking, there are only two important roads: The broad main route from the port, La Savina, in the northwest, to La Mola, in the extreme southeast, and the less-travelled road from Sant Francesc to Cap de Berbería in the south. The longest distance that you will in all probability cover in one go on Formentera is the route from La Savina to La Mola.

Recent excavations of grave-sites indicate that Formentera was settled as early as the second millennium BC. In those days, there were enormous freshwater springs that made the fertile earth here ideal for cultivation of grain. That is why the Romans, who used the island as a granary, called it *Frumentaria,* 'Rich in Grain'. Although the

A beach out of a picture-book: Platja de Mitjorn, on the south coast of Formentera

MARCO POLO SELECTION: FORMENTERA

1 Bob's Lending Library
Whodunits for holiday
reading and books on the
Flower Power movement
(page 88)

2 Fonda Pepe
A breath of the hippie
past (page 88)

3 La Mola
High over the sea, a
monument to the father of
science fiction, Jules Verne
(page 87)

4 Platja de Mitjorn
Broad sand dunes and
excellent bathing
(page 82)

5 Platja Ses Illetas
A heavenly beach
(page 84)

6 Sa Gavina
A fish restaurant right
on the Platja d'es Pujols
featuring specialties
made to local recipes
(page 85)

groundwater has long since dried up, and large-scale growing of grain is no longer possible here, the name has lived on, in altered form.

Around 1400, when North African pirates regularly attacked the island, many residents left Formentera. The island remained practically unpopulated for almost 200 years. It was only when the turbulent situation in the western Mediterranean began to settle down somewhat at the beginning of the 17th century that a gradual repopulation of the island began. Soon afterwards the town of Sant Francesc (formerly San Francisco) was founded. It is still the administrative centre of the island. The main settlement in the area of the harbour at La Savina was Sant Ferràn, which quickly became the second-largest place on Formentera. In the last years of the 20th century both places have forfeited much of their significance and have had to give

way to Es Pujols, which is constantly growing in importance.

ES PUJOLS

(108/C3-4) You may look for the usual fortified church, so common on the Pitiusas, but in Es Pujols, you won't find it. But to make up for this shortcoming, this largest town on the island has all the usual things one takes for granted elsewhere, so that you won't feel that all is lost: Discotheques, bars, night clubs, international restaurants with Indian, Argentinian, and Italian cuisine, and lots of hotels. Until a few years ago all one could expect was the old fishing port, which today is little more than a favourite occasion for a snapshot. The fishermen have moved out. While they don't live here anymore, they still keep their boats at their old port. The lack of older buildings comes as no surprise when one learns that the entire town was laid out according to plan, expressly to accommodate visitors. So can we say that this is an ordinary tourist stronghold? Well, yes, but a small one, even by Formentera standards, and on a human scale. For many years the streets in Es Pujols didn't even have names. Street names since have been introduced, but only here and there, and they haven't completely caught on. They're not really needed here, since you can't get lost in Es Pujols, even on the first day of your holiday. If you do have any problems finding your way, simply ask someone. It is very probable indeed that any passer-by will be an English-speaker, since one finds that many northern and central Europeans are attracted to Es Pujols. They feel quite at home. Many visitors like it so much that they make a second home here.

SIGHTS

Ca Na Costa   (108/B3)
The way to the megalithic graves, only a few km northwest of Es Pujols, is well marked. The gravesite itself was excavated only in 1974, and is in relatively good condition. The discovery of these remains at Ca Na Costa provided the first proof that Formentera was inhabited in prehistoric times. This alone means that this place is one of the most important archeological sites of the Pitiusas.

To get there, leave Es Pujols in the direction of the saltworks. After about one km turn left at the signpost and drive on towards Estany Pudent. The grave

sites are between the salt pans and the road.

Las Salinas   (108/B3)
The saltworks of Formentera have not been profitable for years, but they are worth preserving on ecological grounds alone. This is the only place, for example, where a number of very rare halophytic plants (plants that grow in saltwater and in salty soil) are found. The most beautiful beach on Formentera is just around the corner, the ★ *Platja Ses Illetas*. There is also a restaurant much frequented by celebrities housed in a 200-year-old salt mill, *Es Molí de Sal (Tel. 908 13 67 73; category 1)*. If you wonder why the tables are all full, but the restaurant's parking lot is empty, it's because the owners of the luxury yachts anchored offshore arrive at the door in their rubber boats.

RESTAURANTS

Café de l'Opéra
This café with the French name is in fact a small restaurant that features not only French cuisine, but excellent Catalan food as well. *Open daily except Mon from 6 pm, Es Pujols, no Tel., category 2*

Can Rafalet
⬧⬧ Es Caló is a little clutch of houses on the road to La Mola. There is a small beach here, and the restaurant *Can Rafalet*. From the terrace you have a magnificent view of the northern coast of Formentera. *Open daily 1 pm–3.30 pm; Es Caló; Tel. 971 32 70 16; category 2*

Capri

The best place to sit in this restaurant, a great favourite with everyone for years, is on the terrace, overgrown with climbing plants that provide a grateful shade. *Open daily 1 pm–3 pm and 7 pm–11 pm; Es Pujols; Tel. 971 32 83 52; category 2*

La Formentereña

A cozy comfortable restaurant direct on the beach with good food and generous portions. The specialty is salt chicken. *Open daily 1 pm–3.30 pm and 7 pm–midnight; Platja de Mitjorn, km 9; Tel. 971 32 87 53; category 3*

Gaucho

As the name suggests, we have here an Argentine steak house, whose owner will gladly explain to his patrons what special things go into the preparation of an Argentine steak. Carlos Alberto has been running the restaurant since 1982. *Open daily 7 pm–midnight; C/. Roca Plana, no number; category 2*

Sa Gavina

★ The Seagull rises head and shoulders above the general run of restaurants featuring 'international cuisine'. This outstanding restaurant, the recipient of many culinary prizes, serves up dishes from the repertoire of the Pitiusas and at reasonable prices too. Some of the specialties are *arroz negro* (black rice), *suquet de peix* (different sorts of fish) and *burrida de ratjada* (skate). *Open daily 9 am–midnight; Platja d'es Pujols; Tel. 971 32 83 51; category 2*

La Tortuga

The Turtle isn't on the telephone, so you write out your reservation on a slip of paper and put it in the green letterbox attached to the wall of the restaurant. *La Tortuga* is a bit outside Es Pujols on the road to La Mola. Formentera Pork has been a favourite specialty of the house for years. *Open daily 7.30 pm–11 pm; Carretera La Mola, km 6.6; category 2*

Verdera

This bar on the main road is a particular favourite of the local inhabitants, and for good reason. The stews are outstanding and the *tapas,* too. *Sant Ferràn; category 3*

SHOPPING

A very small artists' market is held every evening on the square in front of the *Hostal Sa Voltá* during the summer months. Before noon it is to be found on the *Placa de sa Constitució* in Sant Ferràn. The things on sale are showy and tempting, but not terribly varied. Apart from this, there isn't much shopping to be done in Es Pujols. If you want to take back an attractive souvenir of Formentera, it's best to go to the artists' market at La Mola, held on Sunday afternoons. The so-called hippies from Ibiza go there, too. *(4 pm–8 pm Sun).*

ACCOMMODATION

Can Rafalet

〰️ The guest house Fonda is in the tiny village of Es Caló, immediately next to the old fishing port. There is a restaurant attached to it, and from its terrace you can enjoy an enchanting view of the north coast of the island. The atmosphere generally is in keeping with the view and the cozy restaurant. *Es Caló; Tel. 608 13 65 92 (mobile); category 3*

Formentera Playa

On the southern side of the island, direct on the splendid Platja de Mitjorn. This is a well-run, above-average, hotel of the mid-range variety. *Platja de Mitjorn; 315 rooms; Tel. 971 32 80 00, Fax 971 32 80 01; category 2*

Hostal Sa Voltá

One can stay here during the winter months as well, since the house has central heating, a rare exception to the general rule on Formentera. The hotel's cafeteria offers one of the best breakfasts on the entire island. *C/. Espalmador (corner Av. Miramar); 18 rooms; Tel. 971 32 81 25; category 2*

Iberotel Club La Mola

This complex on the Platja de Mitjorn, overwhelmingly patronised by northern Europeans, is one of the best places to stay on all Formentera. The villas are outfitted with everything you could possibly desire, including a kitchenette and a fridge. The hotel and club offer practically all water sports, from diving to windsurfing to water skiing. *Platja de Mitjorn; 328 rooms; Tel./Fax 971 32 80 69; category 1*

Mar y Sal

An apartment complex in Ses Salinas. Comfortable one- and two-room apartments with kitchen, television, and roofed terraces. *Ses Salines de Formentera; Tel. 971 32 20 94; category 1*

Roca Plana

This two-star establishment is the equivalent of a well-run pension. It is simply furnished and clean, and in the immediate vicinity of the beach. *Platja d'es Pujols, no number; 40 rooms; Tel. 971 32 83 35, Fax 971 32 86 80; category 3*

Voramar

The alternative to the *Fonda Pepe*, and more or less in the same price category. *Sant Francesc; 47 rooms; Tel. 971 32 86 80, Fax 971 32 84 01; category 3*

SPORTS & LEISURE

The *La Mola* complex offers the best opportunities for those interested in sports. Surfboards can be rented on the Platja d'es Pujols. Cycling is popular everywhere on the island. Hire prices are around 700 pesetas per day, less per day when the rental period is longer. Ten days, for instance, will cost about 6,000 pesetas. Mopeds too are cheaper when you hire one for several days. One day costs 2,000 pesetas, ten days 16,000. One can hire horses at the Club de Hipica de Formentera. *Club de Hipica, Carretera Cap de Berbería; Tel. 971 32 26 38 (about one km from Sant Francesc).* There are tennis courts at the big hotels and club complexes. Most of them cost around 900 pesetas per hour.

ENTERTAINMENT

The nightlife in Es Pujols is limited to one very small area of the town. If you walk towards the sea to the *Capri* restaurant, and pass by the *Truy* restaurant, on your left, you will come to a little pedestrian precinct. The high-flyers of the Formentera night-scene can dance here until the early hours of the morning which, on Formentera, in contrast to Ibiza, means 1 am. There are two smaller discos nearby, the *Tipic* and the *Magoo*, which are hardly worth mentioning, and a jumping rock joint where one can dance till one drops, every night.

Tennis Bar

The best-known local in the bar district of Es Pujols. *Open daily 8 pm–1 am; C/. Espardell*

Zebra

Formerly the *Zebra Art Gallery.* The owners have done away with the 'Art Gallery' part of it to better concentrate on what apparently brings in more people: The loudest music on Formentera. *Open daily 8 pm–3 am; C/. Punta Prima*

INFORMATION

The only tourist-information bureau on the island is in the new buildings of the harbour complex of La Savina. The opening hours of the *Oficina de Información y Turismo* more or less coincide with the arrivals and departures of the ferries. *Port de la Savina; Tel. 971 32 20 57*

SURROUNDING AREA

El Pilar   (109/E5)

The Formenterans carry on their tradition of handicrafts in the little houses of the island's hamlets. If you are interested in hand-knitted pullovers and scarves of genuine Formentera wool, you should take a look in one of the numerous shops.

But there's more than clothing available here. You can also find the famous Formentera sheep's cheese, for one thing. When try this savoury herb-flavoured cheese, be sure to chase it down with a glass of the very dry and tart local wine. El Pilar is 'in' these days, and there is also the *Lighthouse* on the cliffs ★ *La Mola*, which has since 1861 shown the way to passing ships. It has since been transferred to private hands. Here, right on this promontory of the coast, and 192 metres above sea level, stands a monument to the father of science fiction, Jules Verne, erected in 1978. One of his books, 'A Journey Through the Solar System,' mentions Formentera. Don't forget, on the way to El Pilar, to make a brief detour to the *Poblado Romano*, which was discovered at the beginning of the 1980s. It is barely two km before Es Caló, at kilometre-stone 10. It is the remains of a Roman fort, and there is a good system of signs to guide the visitor to it. You will get something for your thirst in ⤷ *Mirador (Carretera La Mola, km 14.2)*, the bar with the best view of the island. In good weather you can see all the way to Cap de Berbería.

Sant Ferràn
de ses Roques   (108/C4)

⚓ Sant Ferràn should really be called San Francisco, after the one-time Californian capital of hippiedom and Flower Power. This town, Sant Ferràn, was the centre of the 'alternative' movement for many young Europeans who never managed to get to the

West Coast of the USA in the days when it was all happening. The ★ lending library run by the American expatriate Bob and the *Fonda Pepe* in the centre of town were the principal meeting-places of the European flower children. In *Bob's Lending Library* there are more than 20,000 volumes in eight languages to choose from. Bob lends them out for a 'suggested contribution' that varies with the thickness of the book in question. *(C/. Major, no number).* Bob himself is a walking history of the hippie era who can tell you all about the 1960s and 1970s on the island, and who is always ready for a friendly chat. The ★ *Fonda Pepe* (*Tel. 971 32 80 33; category 3*) is to be found in the same street, a few houses farther on. Although Pepe has, since his hippie days, entered into contracts with the big travel agencies, the atmosphere of the 1960s still lingers on in the dark rooms of the hotel. The Fonda, as it is affectionately called by its steady customers, has a good reputation as a hotel these days, but does not live on that alone. A piece of the past has survived here, and attracts young people from all over the world who want to see for themselves the places where the spirit of 'anything goes' flourished back then. Not at all far from Sant Francesc, on the road to La Mola, at (*km 6.3*), is the *Cova d'en Xeroni*. Vicente Turmayans will show you, for a minimal but well-spent fee, the caves with stalactites and stalagmites that he disovered in 1975, a unique treasure of Formenteran nature.

Sant Francesc de Formentera (108/B4)

In Sant Francesc, the administrative centre of the island, everything revolves around the central square, the *Plaça de sa Constitució*. Here are the imposing fortified church (18th century) the mayor's office, or town hall, and the Post and Telegraph Office. Everyone who has business with the authorities or with his bank comes to Sant Francesc before noon — and it's also a good opportunity to see who has arrived on the island. At any rate, this is a chance to enjoy the happy, bubbly life of this little town. The *Cafetería del Centro*, directly across from the church, is a great favourite. They rent rooms here as well. (*Tel. 971 32 00 63; category 3*). You can find particularly lovely handmade jewellery at all price levels at *Enric Majoral* (*C/. Luis Salvador, 18*). He specialises in silverwork. You can eat well in the restaurant called *Agua con Gas Es Plá*, a lovely old restored country house in the street that leads to Cala Sahona.*(Open daily from 7 pm; Tel. 971 32 27 90; category 2).* The restaurant specialises in Indian dishes, and there is as well an enormous selection of beers from all over the world. Past Sant Francesc you come to *Cala Sahona*, a small and very quiet bay for swimming, with one of the best hotels on the island, built at the beginning of the 1970s. (*Cala Sahona; 69 rooms; Tel. 971 32 20 30, Fax 971 32 25 09; category 2*). Further towards the south you come across a well-built road to *Cap de Berbería*, the southernmost point of Formentera.

Beaches, fortified churches, isolated villages

These routes are marked in green on the map on the inside front cover and in the Road Atlas beginning on page 100

① THE PRETTIEST BEACHES

 Would three weeks on one and the same bit of sand bore you to tears? Only natural. But this island has more than 56 km of beach, all different, pebbly and sandy, empty and crowded, with shady spots, and, best of all, wide sunny stretches. On the shore of which little bay would you prefer to bask in the rays of the sun? Decide for yourself after this little tour of Ibiza's beaches. Fifty-five km, nine hours.

Let's begin with one of the best-known beaches, the Platja d'en Bossa. Take the Carretera Sant Francesc out of Ibiza City, through Figueretes, towards the south. After about four km, just before the village of Sant Jordi, there's a signposted road off to the left, to the *Platja d'en Bossa (p. 45)*. It is a two-km-long bathing beach along a bay, frequented mainly by families. The beach is broad, of fine sand, with dunes behind it. It is flat, and the bottom slopes gently out to sea, which makes it a good place for children. It is only moderately clean, a state of affairs arising from the fact that in summer it is terribly crowded here. If the crush is too much, one can always move on to the *Platja de ses Salines (p. 45)* or to the neighbouring *Platja d'es Codolar*. You drive through San Jordi towards the airport, to the end of the road. Leave the car there and do the last few metres on foot. The beach is 1.5 km long and up to 30 m wide. It is flat, made of fine sand, with dunes, and clean water. Things here that other beaches don't seem to have are waiter service and a disc-jockey who plays music. Whoever prefers to swim to fewer background decibels should fold his towel, steal away, and spread it instead on the nearby *Platja de sa Caleta*. The road to that beach begins at the airport and goes through Ca'n Torres to Es Codolar. Just after Es Codolar there is a litle dirt road to the beach. This beach, overhung by high cliffs, is not much used, and very quiet.

You'll need sandals or bathing shoes, though, because there isn't much sand here, just a great deal of gravel and stones. That is what makes the water clear. And if you want even more solitude, try the other beaches to right and left. As well as room to spread out, you have a splendid view of Formentera from here. The *Cala d'es Jondal* is just as beautiful, but has more shade. To get there, drive from Sa Caleta by the narrow road to Ca'n Arribas. There is a big parking lot right on the beach where you can leave the car. The beach is lined with pine trees and the plant native to Ibiza known as *savinas* grows there. At any rate, there is plenty of shade. The beach is of fine sand, trucked in from somewhere else. One disadvantage of this beach is that the shore is rocky, and you will need sandals or bathing shoes.

As you think of going on to the next beach, think about lunch as well. The road from the Cala d'es Jondal goes north, past the Cova Santa *(p. 61)*, and brings you to the national route that connects Ibiza City with Sant Josep. Take it towards Sant Josep. Shortly before Sant Josep (km 10) you will find what you are looking for: The restaurant called *Cana Joana (p. 60)*. Good wine is poured to accompany solid Catalan fare on the terrace of this country house, more than 200 years old. The magnificent view out over the green piney landscape doesn't cost anything.

With a fully-loaded stomach and a great urge for a siesta, drive through Sant Josep in the direction of *Cala Vedella*. This is one of the worst cases of overcrowded beach on the entire island, so leave it to the tender mercies of mass tourism and take the well-marked road, at km 13, towards the south, to *Cala d'Hort*. The road is a good one, and the trip to this little beach is worth making anyway. It is enclosed by an imposing ring of cliffs. There is little plant life here, which means that the water is clear. If you're looking for peace and quiet, you'll find it here, before noon at any rate. Word seems to have got around in tourist circles that there is a magnificent panorama to be enjoyed here, the view of the romantic island *Es Vedrá*, which rises dramatically out of the sea to a height of 382 m. Along with its little-sister island, *Vedranell*, Es Vedrá is the subject of a lot of fantastic stories. To believe the local people, a whole series of UFOs has landed there at one time or another, and a lot of ships vanish without trace. Whatever the truth of all this, you leave Ibiza's own Bermuda Triangle by the same way you arrived, and drive past the Cala Vedella and the Punta Llossa to *Cala Molí*, about two km to the north. The bay is only about 100 m wide and has high cliffs behind it. The beach is of fine sand and gravel, and the water is very clean. You can allow yourself a refreshing swim, doze in the sun, and then start thinking about your further nutritional requirements and where you can get your hands on a cold beer. There is a restaurant on the Cala Molí, but it's just as well to take in a bit more scenery at this point. Take the road northwards, past the Cala Tarida, a small beach for the most part terribly crowded, to Port d'es Torrent. At this point you take a small road, approximately two km long, along the coast to *Café del Mar (p. 57)* and enjoy your cold beer on the terrace. There are *tapas* and a view of the sea before you drive back to Ibiza on Route C731.

 While Ibiza is well known as a holiday paradise, few people understand that away from the beaches and the tourist centres there still exists, in the villages and on the farms, an ages-old, almost hidden, culture. Signs of this old culture are to be seen everywhere, in the daily customs of the peasants, in the music, in the folk dances, the costumes, and above all else, in the architecture. Byzantine Greeks, Romans, Phoenicians, and Moors have all left their traces on the island over the course of the centuries. Fifty-seven km, nine hours.

Take Route C733 out of Ibiza City in the direction of Santa Eulària d'es Riu. Turn right after about two km towards a hamlet called *Jesús,* that has a church well worth seeing. Construction began in 1466 and the church was completed in 1549. Inside, you will find a valuable painted panel by Valencian masters of the early Renaissance.

Continue along this little road through a hilly landscape full of with pine trees, until after about four km you come to *Roca Llisa,* a modern settlement more distinguished for its golf course than for its architecture. This place is the starting-point for excursions to the magnificent *calas,* the little coves cut into the coastline, such as *Cala Llonga* and *Cala Blanca,* and on to *Cap Llibrell.*

Keep going north on the same road for four more km until you get to *Santa Eulària d'es Riu.* The main attraction of this little place is its imposing fortified church, on the Puig de Missa. Its builders, who began their work in the 14th century, situated the church on the foundations of a ruined mosque. Around 1568 the church was converted to a fortified installation with semi-round towers for defense. This massive structure is more of a fortress than a church. In early days, the peasants used it as a place of refuge during pirate attacks. The interior, divided into three sections, has large chapels on either side and a stately Baroque main altar.

Santa Eulària owes its additional title to the river Riu de Santa Eulària, which is these days almost completely dried up. A viaduct, a relic of Roman times and still in good shape, spans the river bed. One can walk along the top of the viaduct, which is almost 2,000 years old. The road from Santa Eulària now leads through pine woods and fields towards Sant Carles. (We are now on the Carretera.) The woods and fields provide a pleasant green contrast to the deep blue of the sea. After about five km you arrive at *Sant Carles de Peralta,* where you should make a short stop at the church. The portal and the interior, with its excellent decorated ceilings, are well worth seeing.

After a stop for refreshment at *Anita's Bar (p. 79)* directly across from the church, you drive on to *Cala Sant Vicent (p. 67),* eight km from Sant Carles. The beach is worth a visit. The nearby *Cova d'es Cuilleram (p. 68)* is one of the island's most significant archaeological sites. Everything indicates that the caves here were sacred to the Punic goddess Tanit. The objects discovered here are now in the Archeological Museum in Ibiza City.

If you've had enough history and culture, you can stop now, at Cala Sant Vicent, have some fresh fish in one of the restaurants, and then doze in the sun on the well-tended beach. But if you are still raging for more travel and adventure, take the curving Route C811 towards *Sant Joan de Labritja*. Here you will find the *Church of Sant Joan Baptista*, built in 1785, worth a look. It is a cube-shaped structure with an octagonal cupola. Even more interesting is the fortified hamlet called *Balàfia*, near Sant Llorenc, six km south of Sant Joan on the C733. This tiny place has kept its original character. It is made up of little white houses, and has three fortified towers, built in the 16th century, from which the peasants fought off Turkish invaders. Here, away from the tourist centres, time seems to have stopped.

To finish things in the grand style, take one more small detour, to *Sant Llorenc* with its little chapel dating back to the 18th century, before you drive back to Ibiza City on Route C733.

③ A RURAL IDYLL

 A couple of little white houses, a bar serving the local Ibizan wine, a little chapel, and a tiny shop. There are still villages like this on Ibiza, scarcely disturbed by tourism. Twenty-three km, four hours.

The point of departure is Sant Antoni de Portmany. You drive north along the road that goes to Santa Agnès, and make the first stop after two km. Here is where you can visit the underground *Capilla de Santa Agnès (p. 58)*. It is a chapel set in caves said to have been used as a church as early as the persecutions of the Christians. What is certain is that at one point or another people put up an altar and celebrated the name-day of St Agnès in this place up to the 18th century. Immediately next the chapel there is a very good, if dear, restaurant, the *Sa Capella de Can Basora (p. 53)*. You can always expect to have a magnificent evening meal here. After four kilometres farther to the north you arrive at *Santa Agnès de Corona (p. 58)*. This small village consists of a couple of white houses, a small and simple chapel, and two bars. In the *Bar Cosmi* you can enjoy a glass of the local wine and the reasonably-priced *tapas*. The bucolic peace and quiet plus the view of the Puig d'en Pera are gratis. If you feel steady on your feet, you might take a stroll to the neighbouring village, *Sant Mateu (p. 59)* and back.

After leaving Santa Agnès you drive past fields and pine woods on a good road towards the south, to *Sant Rafel de Forca (p. 49)*. A visit to this little place is especially worthwhile for anyone who likes ceramics. Many artists have set up their workshops here, and if you take a little time and look around carefully, you might be able to pick up a bargain. The drive back to Sant Antoni along the C731 is only a matter of a few minutes.

Practical information

Important addresses and useful information for your trip to Ibiza and Formentera

AMERICAN & BRITISH ENGLISH

Marco Polo travel guides are written in British English. In North America, certain terms and usages deviate from British usage. Some of the more frequently encountered examples are:
baggage for luggage, billion for milliard, cab for taxi, car rental for car hire, drugstore for chemist's, fall for autumn, first floor for groundfloor, freeway/highway for motorway, gas (-oline) for petrol, railroad for railway, restroom for toilet/lavatory, streetcar for tram, subway for underground/tube, toll-free numbers for freephone numbers, trailer for caravan, trunk for boot, vacation for holiday, wait staff for waiting staff (in restaurants etc.), zip code for postal code.

BUSES

Private firms run the bus services on Ibiza and Formentera. The buses serve all the villages and towns on the islands. The bus lines almost without exception radiate outwards from Ibiza City. Travel by bus is exceptionally inexpensive, if not always particularly comfortable. Travelling by bus is well worth while, especially on the main roads. The half-hour journey between Ibiza City and Sant Antoni, for example, costs only 150 pesetas. In Ibiza City the main bus stops are on the *Av. Isidoro Macabich*, in Santa Eulària opposite the tourist information office in the *C/. Mariano Riquer*, and in Sant Antoni on the fishing docks. It doesn't take long to familiarise yourself with the schedules.

CAMPING

Camping just anywhere is not allowed on Ibiza or Formentera. But the authorities will turn a blind eye providing that you and your tent don't stay in one place too long, and you are somewhere where you won't be in the way. The official camping sites charge on average 600 pesetas per peson, tent, and car — not much cheaper than a room in one of the simpler pensions.
Camping Cala Bassa (**100/B-C6**), *Sant Antoni; no Tel.*
Camping Sant Antoni (**101/D6**), *between Sant Antoni and Ciutat Eivissa, km 14; Tel. 971 34 05 36*
Camping Payés (**103/D2**), *in Porti-*

natx, on the road to Ciutat Eivissa;
Tel. 971 30 18 70

Camping Es Caná (**103/E5**),
*between Santa Eulària and Es Caná,
in Es Caná; Tel. 971 33 21 17*

Camping Florida (**103/E5-6**), *C'an
Martina, Punta Arabí, Es Caná
Punta Arabí; Tel. 971 33 11 54*

CAR RENTAL

There are more than 30 car-rental
firms on Ibiza and Formentera.
Compare prices, and remember
that these prices for the most part
do not include insurance or VAT.
So it's always best to make your de-
cision on the basis of the complete price. Although the complete price will generally include
comprehensive insurance, you
should still ask, to make absolutely
sure. A car of the smallest sort (a
Seat Marbella) can cost more than
7,000 pesetas per day at the height
of the season. It is often cheaper to
book a car before you leave home.

CONSULATES & EMBASSIES

American Consulate
*Avda Rey Jaume III 26, 07012
Palma; Tel. 971 72 50 51, 971 72 26
60, Fax 971 71 87 55*

British Consulate
*Plaza Major, 3, 07002, Palma; Tel.
971 71 24 45, Fax 971 71 75 20*

Canadian Embassy
*Núñez de Balboa 35, 28001 Madrid;
Tel. (34) 914 23 250, Fax (34) 914
23 251*

CURRENCY

You will often be asked to show
your passport or other identification when you change money at

a bank *(8.30 am–2 pm Mon–Fri, until 7 pm Thurs)*. Eurocheques and
traveller's cheques in pesetas are
accepted without problems. You
can also change money at the re-
ception desks of the larger hotels,
if at a somewhat less favourable
rate. The most practical way to get
cash is from the automated teller
machines (Eurocard or credit
card). Most large hotels, restaurants, and other businesses accept
the usual credit cards.

CUSTOMS

Non-EU nationals are allowed to
bring into the country up to 200
cigarettes or 50 cigars, up to 1
liter alcohol over 22 proof, and
up to 2 liters of wine.

DRIVING

One seldom sees a car with foreign
plates on Ibiza and Formentera.
The boat trip from the Spanish
mainland to the Pitiusas, long,
complicated, and dear, is worthwhile only if one is planning a long
stay. Instead, people rent cars or,
when speed isn't a consideration, a
moped. The Ibizan roads have
been resurfaced and are well-main-
tained. If, though, you decide to
leave the main highways, you will
need to exercise a certain skill and
care to avoid the frequent potholes
in the smaller roads. Parking is a
great problem in the larger
towns. Be careful here: The Policia
Municipal are seldom content with
a mere fine in cases of illegal parking, but most of the time tow the
car away as well, and that can be expensive. The traffic rules are much
like those in other countries. You
must wear seat belts, and the
blood-alcohol limit is 0.5 milli-

grammes per thousand. The filling stations are open 7 am–9 pm Mon-Sat. There is an emergency source of petrol; the station on the way out of Ibiza City towards Santa Eulària is open at night. But before you can fill up there, you have to pay through the bulletproof glass of the attendant's shelter. If your rental car breaks down, you should get in touch with the car-rental firm right away before contacting the emergency breakdown service. The Guardia Civil as well can assist: *Tel. 971 30 11 00*.

GENERAL ASSISTANCE

Theft, a wretched hotel, other holiday troubles? The distressed can obtain advice from the office of the *Conselleria de Turismo de Ibiza-Formentera* in Ibiza town. *(Av. d'Espanya, 49, Tel. 971 19 59 00, Fax 971 19 59 10, e-mail: cief.general@cief.bitel.es, 9 am-1 pm Mon-Fri)*.

HEALTH

You can call a Red Cross (Cruz Roja) ambulance by dialling the central number *971 39 70 00*. On Formentera you can call a medical service at *971 32 23 69*. The Guardia Civil is at *971 32 20 22* The general emergency number for the police is *092*. If you need medical attention, ask at the desk of your hotel or apply to your tour group, if you are travelling with a group. If they can't provide what you need, ring your vice-consulate in Ibiza.

INFORMATION

Spanish Tourist Office

Canada: *34th floor, 2 Bloor Street West, Toronto, Ontario M5S 1M8,* *Tel. (416) 961 31 31, Fax (416) 961 19 92*

Great Britain: *57-58 St James's St., London SW1A 1LD, Tel. 0891/ 669-920, Fax 0171/ 629- 4257*

USA: *35th floor, 666 Fifth Avenue, New York, NY 10103, Tel. (212) 265 88 22, Fax (212) 265 88 64*

MEASURES & WEIGHTS

1 cm	0.39 inch
1 m	1.09 yd (3.28 ft)
1 km	0.62 miles
1 m²	1.20 yd²
1 ha	2.47 acres
1 km²	0.39 mi²
1 g	0.035 ounces
1 kg	2.21 pounds
British tonne	*1016 kg*
US ton	*907 kg*

1 litre is equivalent to 0.22 Imperial gallons and 0.26 US gallons

NUDE BATHING

Although there are only two official nude-bathing beaches on Ibiza (at Es Cavallet near Ses Salinas and at Aigua Blanca, in the northeast), and only one on Formentera (Ses Illetas), one can swim nude without problems on the more remote beaches.

POST

Stamps can be bought at post offices (*correos*) and from tobacconists (*tabaco, estanco*). Letters and postcards to EU countries presently cost 70 ptas. Post-boxes are yellow.

SCHOOL HOLIDAYS

The Spanish school holidays begin on the 22 June and end

on 15 September. Everyone who goes to Ibiza during the summer should know that the island is an absolute madhouse during this period. One should make one's plans with this in mind.

TELEPHONES

It is better not to call from your hotel room, as rates are very high. Instead, go to a phone box (blue-green) and use your phone card (purchased at the tobacconist). To phone abroad, you need to dial *00* first, then the appropriate country code (for the UK *44,* for the USA and Canada *1,* for Ireland *353*), then the local number. A *reduced rate* applies *daily 10 pm–8 am, Sat 12 noon–Mon 8 am* and on *holidays.* For all phone calls on the island as well as to all other Balearic islands, *971* must be dialled first. Those who bring their mobile phones to the island should obtain information from their provider regarding local and international calls.

TIPPING

The bills in bars and restaurants include something for service. If you want to tip more, 10 % of the total is the usual amout. If you find that too much, give less, or even nothing. No one has thus far actually been put in the stocks on Ibiza for not tipping.

VOLTAGE

The electric current is 220 V practically everywhere.

WATER SPORTS

All imaginable water craft are available for hire or charter on the Ibizan coast, from pedalos to catamarans all the way to sailing yachts and motorboats. The pedalos are available at almost any beach, there are wind-surfing and sailing at all of the larger beaches at least, and whoever doesn't know how to do these things, can learn on the spot. Some of the surfing and sailing places offer courses. A 12-hour beginner's course in windsurfing costs about 25,000 pesetas, a sailing course approximately 30,000. These fees for courses are included in the overall fee paid to some travel agencies.

You'll need a motorboat licence from home to charter a power boat or a sailboat, and of course a little money. Charter prices vary according to the type of boat involved and how it's outfitted. They begin at around 40,000 pesetas. Early booking is advised.

Divers as will find everything they need on Ibiza and Formentera. Diving schools on both islands offer beginner's courses and equipment.

On Ibiza:
Coral Yachting
Ciutat Eivissa, Marina Botafoch;
Tel. 971 31 39 26,
Fax 971 31 37 23
Diving Center Sirena
Sant Antoni, C/. Balanzat 29,
Tel. 971 34 29 66
Free Delphin Diving
Cala Codolar, in Club Delphin;
Tel. 971 80 62 10, Fax 971 80 60 52
Pesca Ibiza
Ciutat Eivissa, Av. 8 de Agosto, Edificio Brisol (next to the Pacha disco);
Tel./Fax 971 31 44 91

Diving School H₂O
*In the El Corso Hotel, Platja Tala-manca (east of Ciutat Eivissa);
Tel./Fax 971 31 35 24*

Motonáutica
Carretera Aeropuerto, km 3.5; Tel. 971 30 66 65, Fax 971 30 66 62

Offshore Sailing
Ciutat Eivissa, Marina Botafoch; Tel. 971 19 07 09, Fax 971 19 04 05
On Formentera:

Náutica Pins
La Savina, Av. Mediterranea 15-19; Tel./Fax 971 32 26 51

WEATHER

The climate of the Pitiusas is more even than that of the other Balearic islands because there are no large mountains here, and no large land mass. The surrounding Mediterranean provides the comfortable temperatures here. There are no large temperature swings, as on the Continent. Even in summer the mercury seldom goes as high as 30° C (86° F), and in the winter months scarcely ever falls under 7° C (45° F).

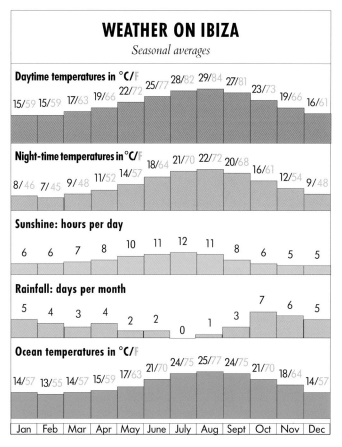

WEATHER ON IBIZA
Seasonal averages

Daytime temperatures in °C/F
15/59 15/59 17/63 19/66 22/72 25/77 28/82 29/84 27/81 23/73 19/66 16/61

Night-time temperatures in °C/F
8/46 7/45 9/48 11/52 14/57 18/64 21/70 22/72 20/68 16/61 12/54 9/48

Sunshine: hours per day
6 6 7 8 10 11 12 11 8 6 5 5

Rainfall: days per month
5 4 3 4 2 2 0 1 3 7 6 5

Ocean temperatures in °C/F
14/57 13/55 14/57 15/59 17/63 21/70 24/75 25/77 24/75 21/70 18/64 14/57

| Jan | Feb | Mar | Apr | May | June | July | Aug | Sept | Oct | Nov | Dec |

Do's and don'ts

*How to avoid some of the traps and pitfalls
that may face the unwary traveller*

Telephoning

If you want to phone home, be sure to do it in one of the call boxes of the Spanish telephone company Telefonica. Avoid making long-distance calls from your hotel, in a restaurant or from a bar. The extra charge these places put on a telephone call is hair-raising.

Disco freebie cards

More often than you would like perhaps, a sweet young thing comes along the street with a twinkle in her eye who presses into your hand a card that promises something free at one of the many discos. You may think at first that you've got lucky, but the truth is, you haven't exactly won the lottery. Our advice is, pitch that card into the first rubbish bin you see and go to some disco worth going to and pay the regular price. Bars and discos that use these so-called freebie cards that promise entry to attract customers are almost never worth it – you have to pay for the drinks anyway. The same goes for the bars that make such offers as 'Two Drinks for the Price of One' – they're simply out to snag customers any way they can. The catch in these deals is that you could easily have two drinks for the same price somewhere else, and perhaps better ones.

Sharks in the harbour

It's not only the African watch-sellers with their 'guaranteed real Rolexes' who troll for innocent tourists along the waterfront of the island's capital city. Watch out as well for the men who in the early hours of the evening set up their little folding tables and move a ball of paper with blinding speed to and fro among three inverted cups. Never, ever, have anything to do with this mug's game. In fact, don't even stand around there. You will only lose your money, either by playing the 'game' or to one of the deft pickpockets who will take advantage of your absorption in the proceedings to lighten your load.

Dogs

No, they're not dangerous, but uncommonly friendly and sociable. We speak of Ibiza's stray dogs. It's not wise to pet them, or they will dog your steps throughout your entire holiday. Their fleas too.

Road Atlas of Ibiza/Formentera

*Please refer to back cover for an overview
of this Road Atlas*

	A	B	C

1

3 km

2

MAR

MEDITERRÀNIA

3

4

S'EIVISSA
I. IBIZA

Cap N

5

sa Forac

S'A

Cala

Punta de sa Ga

Cap Negre

Cala Grassió

Cap d'es Cavall

Cap Blar

Dénia 4 h   Cap de s' Aguila   *ILLA DE SA CONILLERA*   Badia de Sant A

Cala

I. BLEDA PLANA

6

I.BLEDA REDONDA   Cap Blanc   Punta de sa Torre   Punta Xinxó

Cala Roig   Cap la Bassa

I. DES BOSC

Cala Bassa

I. NA GORRA

104

100

I. DE S'ESPARTOR   Cala Con

Cala Bassa   Port d'es Torrent

Punta

Platja d'es Port

ta de
alera

Portinatx

Punta d'es Gat

Cala d'en Serra

Raco de sa Talaia

iuda

sa Punta
Verde

SES FORMIGUES

Cala del Jonc

Talaia de Sant Vicent

Cova
d'es Culleran

Clot d'es Llamp

an de
abritja

303

PM-811

Cala de
Sant Vicent

Punta Grossa

(73)

Sant Vicent
de sa Cala

2,5

Cala de Sant Vicent ★

erra de la Mala Costa

6

Platja d'es Figueral

es Figueral

Ximalна

ILLOT DE S' HORT

8

PM-810

Sant Carles
de Peralta

Punta Verde

Cala d'es Pou
d'es Lleó

3

(74)

Talaia de Sant Carles

230 5

Punta
d'en Valls

ILLA DE
TAGOMAGO

2

Mina
de Plomo

Ca'n Jordi

Ca'n Fulgencio

3

Cap Roig

Cala Mastella

Ca'n
Pep Mari

s'Argentera

2,5

Club Cala Llenya

La Joya

Punta d'en Ribes

Cala Llenya

Cala Nova

Cala Nova

4,5

es 'Cana

Platja d'es Canar

bas

218

1,5

Cala
Pada

2,5

Punta Arabí

s'Argamassa

2

Cala Pada

Punta Arabí

a d'es Puig

Missa

Punta d'es
Faralló

I. DE SANTA EULÀRIA

I. REDONA

Platges de Sta. Eulària

3 km

Santa Eulària d'es Riu

Arboles

Punta Blanca

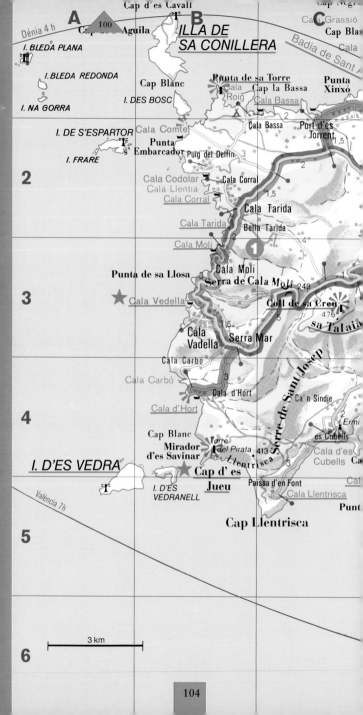

Cap d'es Cavall

A 100 **B** ILLA DE **C** Cap Negr

Dénia 4 h SA CONILLERA Cala Grassió

Cap de s'Aguila Cap Bla

I. BLEDA PLANA Badia de Sant

I. BLEDA REDONDA Cap Blanc **Punta de sa Torre** **Punta**

I. DES BOSC Cala Roig Cap la Bassa **Xinxó**

I. NA GORRA Cala Bassa

I. DE S'ESPARTOR Cala Comte Cala Bassa Port d'es

Punta Torrent

s' Embarcador Puig del Delfín 3

I. FRARE 2 1,5

2 Cala Codolar Cala Corral

Cala Llentia 1,5

Cala Corral **Cala Tarida**

Cala Tarida Bella Tarida

Cala Moli 4

2

Punta de sa Llosa 3 **Cala Molí**

Serra de Cala Molí 248

3 Cala Vedella **Coll de sa Creu**

476

Cala 1,5 5 **sa Talaia**

Vadella **Serra Mar**

Cala Carbó

Cala Carbó 3 Ca'n Sindie

Cala d'Hort **Ermi

4 es Cubells

Cap Blanc Torre Cala d'es Ca

Mirador del Pirata 413 Cubells

d'es Savinar Llentrisca 3 Cal

I. D'ES VEDRA **Cap d'es** Paissa d'en Font

Jueu Cala Llentrisca

I. D'ES **Punt

València 7h VEDRANELL*

Cap Llentrisca

5

6 3 km

104

② D · 1,5 E 103 F

Dala
Pada · 2 · s'Argamassa
Cala Pada · Punta Arabí
d'es Puig · Punta d'es · Punta Arabí
Missa · Farralló · ◠ I. DE SANTA EULÀRIA
Platges de Sta. Eulària · ◦ I. REDONA

Barcelona 10 h

1

Santa Eulària d'es Riu

rboles

Punta Blanca

2

ga

Punta Rotja

C.Llonga

Torretes

Llibrell

rrà

Palma (Ciutat de Mallorca) 4½ h

3

4

M A R

5

E D I T E R R À N I A

6

3 km

109

A IS. NEGRES
105
EL. D'ES PENJATS
Far d'es Penjats
B
C

1
Far d'en Pou
I. D'ES PORCS
I. DE SA TORRETA
Cala Boix
Cala Torretes
I. D

Port de
s'Espalmador
I. DE S'ESPALMADOR
Punta de Gastavi
Punta del Ras

2
Trucadors
Dénia 4 h, Gandia 5 h
Platja Illetats
Racó de ses Ampolles
I. POUET
I. RODONA
es Cavall d'en Borràs

3
**Punta de sa
Pedrera**
ses Selines
2,5
Platja d'es Pujols
sa Savina
Cala Savina
Ca'n Miquel
de Baix
Punta P
Punta del Bandil
es Banc
Estany
d'es Peix
Estany
Pudent
es Pujols
Racó d'es
Torre de sa
Gavina
Ca'n Maianset 3
2,5
**Punta de sa
Gavina**
Ca'n Bartomevet
2,5
St. Ferràn de ses F

4
2
Església de
St-FrancescXavier
Cova d'en Jeroni
Ses Roques
Caló d'es Trui
**St. Francesc
de Formentera**
es Ca
Marí
Cala Saona
F o r m e n t e r a
1,5
2
Punta Rossa
Ca'n Pujol
del Fum
3
2,5
Torre d'es
Pi d'es
Català
Ca'n Vicent Pins
Racó
de s' Argelà
Platja
de Mitjorn

5
2
Cap Alt
1,5
Cà La Coixa
Parra
Ca'n Petit
Platja de
113
Torre
Punta de s'Aguila
Racó de s'Alga
4,5
es Plà del Rei
104

6
Torre d'es Cap de Barbaria
Cap de Barbaria

108

1

ARDELL

M A R

2

M E D I T E R R À N I A

3

4

I. FORMENTERA

Punta de sa
Palmera   Punta de sa Creu

enyal d'en Jaume

sa Cala

Ferrer   Punta d'en Joan Jai

es Caló de St. Agusti   Racó
d'es
Calo   Cova
d'es Fum 133   es Monestir   Punta de sa Xindria
sa Xindria

2.5   2.5   Racó de sa Xindria

Mar y Land
la Mola   ⚓   ⚓ N. S. del Pilar   2

5.5   del Pilar
de la Mola   146   Far de la Mola

192   Punta de sa Ruda

Mola   2

d'es Mort   Cala Codolar
es Ram

s'Estufador   Punta Roja

5

|—————— 3 km ——————|

6

ROAD ATLAS LEGEND

Autobahn · Gebührenpflichtige Anschlußstelle · Gebührenstelle · Anschlußstelle mit Nummer · Rasthaus mit Übernachtung · Raststätte · Erfrischungsstelle · Tankstelle · Parkplatz mit und ohne WC		Motorway · Toll junction · Toll station · Junction with number · Motel · Restaurant · Snackbar · Filling-station · Parking place with and without WC
Autobahn in Bau und geplant mit Datum der Verkehrsübergabe	Datum — Date	Motorway under construction and projected with completion date
Zweibahnige Straße (4-spurig)		Dual carriageway (4 lanes)
Bundesstraße · Straßennummern	14 E45	Federal road · Road numbers
Wichtige Hauptstraße		Important main road
Hauptstraße · Tunnel · Brücke	)=(	Main road · Tunnel · Bridge
Nebenstraßen		Minor roads
Fahrweg · Fußweg		Track · Footpath
Wanderweg (Auswahl)		Tourist footpath (selection)
Eisenbahn mit Fernverkehr		Main line railway
Zahnradbahn, Standseilbahn		Rack-railway, funicular
Kabinenschwebebahn · Sessellift		Aerial cableway · Chair-lift
Autofähre		Car ferry
Personenfähre		Passenger ferry
Schiffahrtslinie		Shipping route
Naturschutzgebiet · Sperrgebiet		Nature reserve · Prohibited area
Nationalpark, Naturpark · Wald		National park, natural park · Forest
Straße für Kfz gesperrt	X X X X	Road closed to motor vehicles
Straße mit Gebühr		Toll road
Straße mit Wintersperre	XII-II	Road closed in winter
Straße für Wohnanhänger gesperrt bzw. nicht empfehlenswert		Road closed or not recommended for caravans
Touristenstraße · Paß	Weinstraße 1510	Tourist route · Pass
Schöner Ausblick · Rundblick · Landschaftlich bes. schöne Strecke		Scenic view · Panoramic view · Route with beautiful scenery
Golfplatz · Schwimmbad		Golf-course · Swimming pool
Ferienzeltplatz · Zeltplatz		Holiday camp · Transit camp
Jugendherberge · Sprungschanze		Youth hostel · Ski jump
Kirche im Ort, freistehend · Kapelle		Church · Chapel
Kloster · Klosterruine		Monastery · Monastery ruin
Schloß, Burg · Schloß-, Burgruine		Palace, castle · Ruin
Turm · Funk-, Fernsehturm		Tower · Radio-, TV-tower
Leuchtturm · Kraftwerk		Lighthouse · Power station
Wasserfall · Schleuse		Waterfall · Lock
Bauwerk · Marktplatz, Areal		Important building · Market place, area
Ausgrabungs- u. Ruinenstätte · Feldkreuz		Arch. excavation, ruins · Calvary
Dolmen · Menhir		Dolmen · Menhir
Hünen-, Hügelgrab · Soldatenfriedhof		Cairn · Military cemetery
Hotel, Gasthaus, Berghütte · Höhle		Hotel, inn, refuge · Cave

Kultur
Malerisches Ortsbild · Ortshöhe — **WIEN** (171)

★★ **MILANO** — Eine Reise wert

★ **TEMPLIN** — Lohnt einen Umweg

Andermatt — Sehenswert

Culture
Picturesque town · Elevation

Worth a journey

Worth a detour

Worth seeing

Landschaft
Eine Reise wert — ★★ Las Cañadas

Lohnt einen Umweg — ★ Texel

Sehenswert — Dikti

Landscape
Worth a journey

Worth a detour

Worth seeing

3 km

INDEX

This index lists all the main sights, museums, restaurants and hotels mentioned in this guide. Numbers in bold indicate a main entry, italics a photograph. The articles (en, es, sa, s', las, los, and so on) and particles (de, d', etc.,) are not taken into consideration in the alphabetisation.

What do you get for your money?

 100 pesetas is just about 65 U.S. cents, and one U.S. dollar is about 155 pesetas. It is true that the decline of the peseta has meant a certain financial advantage for tourists from outside the country, but this sort of thinking can be deceptive. The prices in all parts of the Iberian Peninsula have at the same time risen steeply. The Balearics, like the rest of the country, are no longer an inexpensive destination. Some examples will suffice: A cup of café con leche will cost you at least 150 pesetas, a complete breakfast 500 pesetas, a three-course meal in an average restaurant around 3,000 pesetas, a beer in an ordinary bar 200 pesetas, a cocktail anywhere along the waterfront of Ibiza Citys 900 pesetas. It's always cheaper to drink at the bar than at a table, and cheaper inside than outside. To get into one of the superdiscos will set you back about 4,000 pesetas, cocktails another 1,500, and a taxi home, from for example Amnesia to Platja d'en Bossa, 1,500 pesetas. One of the 'with it' people who visits two or three discos in an evening will easily spend 15,000 pesetas. On the other hand, the simpler pleasures are always cheaper. A bus journey from Ibiza City to Sant Antoni costs 150 pesetas, a four-minute telephone call back home about 1,000 pesetas, and postage for postcards and letters, 70 pesetas.

US$	Spanish pesetas (ptas)	£	Spanish pesetas (ptas)	Can$	Spanish pesetas (ptas)
1	155	1	250	1	103
2	310	2	499	2	205
3	465	3	750	3	308
4	620	4	999	4	411
5	776	5	1,248	5	513
10	1,551	10	2,497	10	1,026
15	2,327	15	3,745	15	1,539
20	3,102	20	4,994	20	2,053
25	3,878	25	6,242	25	2,567
30	4,653	30	7,490	30	3,079
40	6,204	40	9,987	40	4,105
50	7,755	50	12,484	50	5,131
60	9,307	60	14,981	60	6,158
70	10,858	70	17,478	70	7,184
80	12,409	80	19,974	80	8,210
90	13,960	90	22,471	90	9,236
100	15,511	100	24,968	100	10,263
200	31,022	200	49,936	200	20,526
300	46,533	300	74,904	300	30,788
400	62,044	400	99,872	400	41,051
500	77,555	500	124,839	500	51,314
750	116,332	750	187,259	750	76,971
1,000	155,110	1,000	249,679	1,000	102,627